Descendants of Levi Davis

Generation 1

1. **LEVI**[1] **DAVIS** was born on 01 Jul 1805 in Loudoun County, Virginia. He died on 06 Jun 1885 in Falls Township, Hocking County, Ohio. He married Mary Ann Rodman on 15 Aug 1830 in Muskingum County, ohio. She was born about 1812 in Pennsylvania. She died on 01 Dec 1886 in Falls Township, Hocking County, Ohio.

More About Levi Davis:
Occupation: 1850 in Falls Township, Hocking County, Ohio; Surveyor and Farmer
Occupation: 1860 in Falls Township, Hocking County, Ohio; Surveyor
Occupation: 1870 in Falls Township, Hocking County, Ohio; Surveyor
Occupation: 1880 in Falls Township, Hocking County, Ohio; Engineer

Notes for Levi Davis:
        (from chapter 36, 1883 History of Hocking Valley)
Levi Davis, civil engineer and surveyor, of Hocking County,
was born in Loudoun County, Va., near Leesburg, July 1, 1805, a
son of John W. and Elizabeth (Hesser) Davis. When he was nine
years of age his parents moved to Fairfax County, Va., remaining
there four years, when they removed to Prince William County, and
three years later returned to Loudoun County. In 1823 they came to
Ohio, first settling near Hanover, Columbiana County. Mr. Davis
received his rudimentary education in the common schools, but by
private personal application acquired a mathemat-ical and scientific
education, and after years of careful study, ob-tained a practical
knowledge of civil engineering and surveying, being one of the best
of that profession in the State. When twenty years of age he left
home and was employed as a laborer on the
public works of the Ohio Canal six months, when he was appointed
superintendent of the canal construction, retaining that position
till 1830. The next three years he was a contractor on the National
turnpike road in Muskingum County, and in 1833 was appointed by
the Government as superintendent of construction for a section of
fifteen miles of the same turnpike in Licking and Franklin counties. In
1836 he resigned his position and was a contractor on the Sandy
and Beaver Canal in Columbiana County till 1838, when he was
employed as superintendent of construction on the slack water
works of Muskingum River till 1839. From that year till 1842 he
taught school in Muskingum County, when he came to Hocking
County and settled two miles south of Logan, where he still resides.
In 1844 he was elected County Surveyor of Hocking County, holding
the position thirty years, when, in 1874, on ac-count of his age, he
declined re-election, and his son, James W., was elected in his
stead. Aug. 15, 1830, Mr. Davis married Mary Ann Rodman, of
Muskingum County. They have had a family of thirteen children,
eight of whom are still living---John R., born Aug. 15, 1831; Sarah J.,
Oct. 5, 1833, now Mrs. John Shields; Samuel G., born March 12,
1835, died Nov. 9, 1836; Wesley A., born July 18, 1837; Levi, May
11, 1839, married Mary Bigham; Mary R., born May 5, 1841, died
May 13, 1841; Lycurgus, born April 3, 1842; James W., July 4,
1844; Eliza A., Nov. 20, 1846; Samantha (Mrs. Jones), May 7, 1849,
died in 1880; Edith C., born April 3, 1852, died April 7, 1854; Harriet
M., born Feb. 18, 1855; Lucellus, Oct. 30, 1859, died Sept. 22,
1863.

Age at death on death record would give birth date of June 12, 1805.

Notes for Mary Ann Rodman:
A second death record gives her date of death as November 30, 1886 in Laurel Township, Hocking County, Ohio, married and born about 1812 in Pennsylvania.

The December 1, 1886 Falls Township, Hocking County, Ohio death record lists her as widowed and born about 1812 in Pennsylvania.

Levi Davis and Mary Ann Rodman had the following children:

i.   JOHN R.[2] DAVIS was born on 15 Aug 1831 in Ohio.

2.   ii. SARAH JANE DAVIS was born on 05 Oct 1833 in Ohio. She died after 13 Jun 1900. She married (1) JOHN SHIELDS before 15 Jun 1880. He was born about 1831 in Ohio. He died on 22 Jun 1886 in Ward Township, Hocking County, Ohio. She married (2) ELI WESTENHAVER on 03 Aug 1848 in Hocking County, Ohio. He was born about 1825 in Ohio. She married (3) GEORGE B. OTIS on 17 Dec 1855 in Hocking County, Ohio. He was born about 1835 in New York.

iii.   SAMUEL G. DAVIS was born on 12 Mar 1835 in Ohio. He died on 09 Nov 1836 in Ohio.

3.   iv. WESLEY A. DAVIS was born on 18 Jul 1837 in Ohio. He married Nancy Barstow on 12 Sep 1861 in Hocking County, Ohio. She was born about 1838 in Ohio.

4.   v. LEVI DAVIS was born on 11 May 1839 in Muskingum County, ohio. He died on 08 Apr 1909 in Perry Township, Hocking County, Ohio. He married (1) MARY ANN BIGHAM, daughter of Isaac Bigham and Mary Elizabeth Delong on 10 Mar 1875 in Hocking County, Ohio. She was born on 15 Feb 1855 in Hocking County, Ohio. She died on 07 Aug 1924 in Greenfield Township, Fairfield County, Ohio. He married (2) MARY B. SHULTZ, daughter of David Shultz and Mary J. Biers on 13 Oct 1859 in Hocking County, Ohio. She was born in 1839 in Ohio. She died on 05 May 1874 in Muskingum County, Ohio.

vi.   MARY R. DAVIS was born on 05 May 1841 in Ohio. She died on 13 May 1841 in Ohio.

5.   vii. LYCURGUS DAVIS was born on 03 Apr 1842 in Ohio. He died on 07 May 1895 in Zanesville, Muskingum County, Ohio. He married (1) EMALINE BARTHOLOW on 16 Aug 1866 in Hocking County, Ohio. She was born about 1851 in Ohio. He married (2) MATTIE JOHNSON on 12 Jun 1887 in Muskingum County, Ohio. She was born in Oct 1848 in Ohio.

6.   viii. JAMES WILLIAM DAVIS was born on 04 Jul 1844 in Logan, Falls Township, Hocking County, Ohio. He died on 13 Nov 1904 in Logan, Hocking County, Ohio. He married Almeda A. Main, daughter of William Main and Belinda Green on 11 Sep 1866 in Hocking County, Ohio. She was born on 29 Apr 1849 in Logan, Falls Township, Hocking County, Ohio. She died on 30 Jan 1928 in Logan, Hocking County, Ohio.

7.   ix. ELIZA A. DAVIS was born on 20 Nov 1846 in Logan, Hocking county, OhioOhio. She married (1) JOHN W. SNIFF, son of Isaiah Sniff and Elizabeth Moore on 25 Dec 1866 in Hocking County, Ohio. He was born on 13 Feb 1842 in Vinton County, Ohio. He died on 16 Jan 1904 in Falls Township, Hocking County, Ohio. She married (2) CHARLES SIMPSON, son of Charles Simpson and Jemima Sutton on 10 Apr 1908 in

Hocking County, Ohio. He was born on 31 Mar 1853 in Pittsburgh, Allegheny County, Pennsylvania.

x.   SAMANTHA DAVIS was born on 07 May 1849 in Ohio. She died in 1880. She married (UNKNOWN) JONES.

xi.   EDITH C. DAVIS was born on 03 Apr 1852 in Ohio. She died on 07 Apr 1854 in Ohio.

xii.   HARRIET M. DAVIS was born on 18 Feb 1855 in Ohio. She died on 16 Nov 1880.

xiii.   LUCELLUS DAVIS was born on 30 Oct 1859 in Ohio. He died on 22 Sep 1863.

Generation 2

2.   SARAH JANE^2 DAVIS (Levi^1) was born on 05 Oct 1833 in Ohio. She died after 13 Jun 1900. She married (1) JOHN SHIELDS before 15 Jun 1880. He was born about 1831 in Ohio. He died on 22 Jun 1886 in Ward Township, Hocking County, Ohio. She married (2) ELI WESTENHAVER on 03 Aug 1848 in Hocking County, Ohio. He was born about 1825 in Ohio. She married (3) GEORGE B. OTIS on 17 Dec 1855 in Hocking County, Ohio. He was born about 1835 in New York.

More About Sarah Jane Davis:
Living In: 1900 With her step son, Curtis Shields, in Carbon Hill Precinct, Ward Township, Hocking County, Ohio.

More About John Shields:
Occupation: 1880 in Ward Township, Hocking County, Ohio; Butcher

More About Eli Westenhaver:
Living In: 1850 Green Township, Hocking County, Ohio

More About George B. Otis:
Occupation: 1860 in York Township, Athens County, Ohio; Coal Rigger
Occupation: 1880 in Ward Township, Hocking County, Ohio; Coal Miner

George B. Otis and Sarah Jane Davis had the following children:
i.   CLARA J.^{3} OTIS was born on 26 Oct 1856 in Logan, Hocking County, Ohio. She died on 26 Mar 1926 in Smithfield, Jefferson County, Ohio. She married J. W. HARTLEY.

More About Clara J. Otis:
Burial: 30 Mar 1926 in Smithfield, Jefferson County, Ohio

ii.   JAMES J. OTIS was born about 1859 in Ohio.

iii.   JOHN OTIS was born about 1863 in Ohio.

iv.   CURTIS OTIS was born in Jan 1866 in Ohio.

More About Curtis Otis:
Living In: 1880 With his mother and step father in Ward Township, Hocking County, Ohio.
Occupation: 1900 in Carbon Hill Precinct, Ward Township, Hocking County, Ohio; Coal Miner

3.   **WESLEY A.**[2] **DAVIS** (Levi[1]) was born on 18 Jul 1837 in Ohio. He married Nancy Barstow on 12 Sep 1861 in Hocking County, Ohio. She was born about 1838 in Ohio.

More About Wesley A. Davis:
Occupation: 1870 in Green Township, Hocking County, Ohio; Farmer
Living In: 1870 With his parents in Falls Township, Hocking County, Ohio.

Wesley A. Davis and Nancy Barstow had the following children:

     i.   WILLIAM[3] DAVIS was born about 1862 in Ohio.

     ii.   LILLIAN MAE DAVIS was born on 18 Feb 1865 in Union Furnace, Hocking County, Ohio. She died on 26 Sep 1941 in Nelsonville, Athens County, Ohio. She married CARMEN CALL.

           More About Lillian Mae Davis:
           Burial: 29 Sep 1941 in Green Lawn Cemetery

4.   **LEVI**[2] **DAVIS** (Levi[1]) was born on 11 May 1839 in Muskingum County, ohio. He died on 08 Apr 1909 in Perry Township, Hocking County, Ohio. He married (1) **MARY ANN BIGHAM**, daughter of Isaac Bigham and Mary Elizabeth Delong on 10 Mar 1875 in Hocking County, Ohio. She was born on 15 Feb 1855 in Hocking County, Ohio. She died on 07 Aug 1924 in Greenfield Township, Fairfield County, Ohio. He married (2) **MARY B. SHULTZ**, daughter of David Shultz and Mary J. Biers on 13 Oct 1859 in Hocking County, Ohio. She was born in 1839 in Ohio. She died on 05 May 1874 in Muskingum County, Ohio.

More About Levi Davis:
Occupation: 1860 in Falls Township, Hocking County, Ohio; Farmer
Living In: 1860 Levi and Mary are living next door to his father in Falls Township, Hocking County, Ohio.
Military Service: Bet. 02 Jul 1861-02 May 1862 ; Company C. 26th Ohio Infantry, U.S. Army
Occupation: 1870 in Hopewell Township, Muskingum County, Ohio; Works on Farm
Living In: 1870 Levi and Mary are living next door to her brother, David Shultz, in Hopewell Township, Muskingum County, Ohio.
Occupation: 1880 in Falls Township, Hocking County, Ohio; Minister
Occupation: 1900 in Laurel Township, Hocking County, Ohio; Farmer
Burial: 10 Apr 1909 in Pisqah Church Cemetery, Hocking County,
Ohio Cause Of Death: Bronchial Pneumonia

More About Mary Ann Bigham:
Living In: 1924 Lancaster, Fairfield County, Ohio
Burial: 10 Aug 1924 in Pisqah Church Cemetery, Hocking County,
Ohio
Cause Of Death: Addisons Disease

Levi Davis and Mary Ann Bigham had the following children:

     i.   LEVI[3] DAVIS was born on 16 Nov 1875 in Falls Township, Hocking County, Ohio. He died on 13 May 1961 in Hocking County, Ohio. He married Emma Louise Springer, daughter of Edward Springer and Caroline Bailey on 29 Dec 1901 in Hocking County, Ohio. She was born on 25 Feb 1882 in Hocking County, Ohio. She died on 26 Jan 1982 in Circleville, Pickaway County, Ohio.

           More About Levi Davis:
           Living In: 1900 With his parents in Laurel Township, Hocking County, Ohio.

Occupation: 1900 in Laurel Township, Hocking County, Ohio; Day Laborer
Occupation: 1901 in Rockbridge, Hocking County, Ohio; Saw Mill Hand
Occupation: 1910 in Perry Township, Hocking County, Ohio; Farmer
Occupation: 1920 in Laurel Township, Hocking County, Ohio; Farmer
Occupation: 1930 in Laurel Township, Hocking County, Ohio; Farmer
Occupation: 1940 in Laurel Township, Hocking County, Ohio; Farmer
Burial: Pisgah Church Cemetery, Hocking County, Ohio

Notes for Levi Davis:
Never had children.

Birth record has birth date of November 30, 1875. Marriage license has birth date of November 16, 1875. World War One draft registration has birth date of November 16, 1875.

----

8.   ii. HARRIETT DAVIS was born on 05 Apr 1876 in Laurel Township, Hocking County, Ohio. She died on 20 Aug 1950 in Oakland, Alameda County, California. She married Elza Allen Doss on 26 May 1895 in Pickaway County, Ohio. He was born on 11 Feb 1873 in Crawford County, Kansas. He died on 23 Aug 1956 in Oakland, Alameda County, California.

    iii. ISAAC WESLEY DAVIS was born on 12 Jan 1879 in Logan, Ohio. He died on 22 Sep 1900.

More About Isaac Wesley Davis:
Occupation: 1900 in Laurel Township, Hocking County, Ohio; Day Laborer
Burial: Pisgah Church Cemetery, Hocking County, Ohio

9.   iv. LYCURGUS DAVIS was born on 18 Oct 1880 in Falls Township, Hocking County, Ohio. He died on 14 Apr 1928 in Columbus, Franklin County, Ohio. He married Myrtle Chambers, daughter of Alexander Chambers and Ellen C. Lendennen on 29 Apr 1903 in Logan, Hocking County, Ohio. She was born on 23 Feb 1880 in Laurel Township, Hocking County, Ohio.

10.   v. SAMUEL BIGHAM DAVIS was born on 07 Dec 1882 in Sunset, Hocking County, Ohio. He died on 19 Dec 1976 in Bucyrus, Crawford County, Ohio. He married Effie E. Gwartney, daughter of Emmet Gwartney and Margaret Williams on 30 Nov 1905 in Lancaster, Ohio. She was born on 25 Apr 1885 in Perry Township, Hocking County, Ohio. She died on 02 Feb 1961 in Columbus, Franklin County, Ohio.

    vi. GEORGE H. DAVIS was born in Apr 1884 in Hocking County, Ohio.

More About George H. Davis:
Occupation: 1900 in Laurel Township, Hocking County, Ohio; Farm Laborer

11.   vii. SARAH DELL DAVIS was born on 24 Dec 1885 in Laurel Township, Hocking County, Ohio. She died on 01 Nov 1957 in Athens, Ohio. She married Daniel Bailey, son of Charles Bailey and Christena Deischle on 28 Dec 1905 in Hocking County, Ohio. He was born on 02 Nov 1875 in Rockbridge, Good Hope Township, Hocking County, Ohio. He died on 20 Dec 1956 in Logan, Ohio.

12.   viii. MARY ANN DAVIS was born on 16 Mar 1887 in Laurel Township, Hocking County,

Ohio. She died on 11 Mar 1971 in Lakeland, Polk County, Florida. She married William Edward Tucker, son of Hollis Clark Tucker and Clara Fox on 29 Jun 1906 in Lancaster, Ohio. He was born on 08 Nov 1885 in Rockbridge, Ohio. He died on 21 Apr 1975 in Plant City, Florida.

13. ix. ESENA BELL DAVIS was born on 05 Jun 1889 in Hocking County, Ohio. She died on 15 Jul 1982 in Columbus, Franklin County, Ohio. She married Wilmer Joseph Jackson, son of Joseph Jackson and Ida Bell on 03 Mar 1906. He was born on 14 Aug 1886 in Sugar Grove, Franklin County, Ohio. He died on 18 Sep 1969 in Columbus, Ohio.

 xi. CHARLES DAVIS was born on 10 Jan 1891 in Laurel Township, Hocking County, Ohio. He died on 15 Jan 1891.

 More About Charles Davis:
 Burial: Pisgah Church Cemetery, Hocking County, Ohio

 Notes for Charles Davis:
 Cemetery survey gives birth date of December 5, 1890 and death date of December 10, 1890. Birth record shows birth date of January 10, 1891.

 ----

14. xi. LYDA JANE DAVIS was born on 25 Dec 1891 in Laurel Township, Hocking County, Ohio. She died on 25 Nov 1981 in Lancaster, Fairfield County, Ohio. She married Anthony Shonk, son of Arron Shonk and Catherine Wohlsheid on 15 Jul 1912. He was born on 14 Jan 1877 in Madison Township, Fairfield County, Ohio. He died on 20 Oct 1943 in Lancaster, Fairfield County, Ohio.

 xii. MINNIE DAVIS was born on 03 Oct 1893 in Hocking County, Ohio. She died on 08 Aug 1894 in Hocking County, Ohio.

 More About Minnie Davis:
 Burial: Pisgah Church Cemetery, Hocking County, Ohio

15. xiii. NELSON B. DAVIS was born on 01 Jul 1895 in Laurel Township, Hocking County, Ohio. He died on 06 Nov 1978 in Fairfield County, Ohio. He married Helen Carrie Kane, daughter of Salem Kane and Mattie Wilson on 19 Jul 1919. She was born on 28 Aug 1901 in Hocking County, Ohio. She died on 01 May 1978 in Lancaster, Fairfield County, Ohio.

More About Mary B. Shultz:
Living In: 1874 in Falls Township, Hocking County, Ohio

5. LYCURGUS[2] DAVIS (Levi[1]) was born on 03 Apr 1842 in Ohio. He died on 07 May 1895 in Zanesville, Muskingum County, Ohio. He married (1) EMALINE BARTHOLOW on 16 Aug 1866 in Hocking County, Ohio. She was born about 1851 in Ohio. He married (2) MATTIE JOHNSON on 12 Jun 1887 in Muskingum County, Ohio. She was born in Oct 1848 in Ohio.

More About Lycurgus Davis:
Military Service: Bet. 21 Oct 1861-08 Jul 1865 ; Company H, 63rd Ohio Infantry, U. S. Army
Occupation: 1870 in Hopewell Township, Muskingum County, Ohio; Laborer
Occupation: 1880 in Falls Township, Hocking County, Ohio; Laborer

Burial: Greenwood Cemetery, Zanesville, Muskingum County, Ohio

Notes for Lycurgus Davis:
Only his daughter, Bella, is living with him in 1880. His son, Charles, is boarding with
Savina Shultz. His wife is not mentioned in the 1880 census report.

Mustered out of Company H, 63rd Ohio Infantry on July 8, 1865 at Louisville, Kentucky.

Lycurgus Davis and Emaline Bartholow had the following children:

     i.   CHARLES ALVIN[3] DAVIS was born on 20 Jan 1869 in Logan, Hocking County,
          Ohio. He died on 26 Mar 1950 in Hopewell Township, Muskingum County, Ohio.

          More About Charles Alvin Davis:
          Living In: 1880 Living as a boarder with Savina Shultz in Falls Township, Hocking
          County, Ohio.
          Burial: 28 Mar 1950
          Occupation: Coal Miner

     ii.   BELLA DAVIS was born on 09 Jun 1871 in Muskingum County, Ohio.

More About Mattie Johnson:
Living In: 1900 Zanesville, Muskingum County, Ohio
Living In: 1920 With her niece, Minnie Craig, in Zanesville, Muskingum County, Ohio.

6.   JAMES WILLIAM[2] DAVIS (Levi[1]) was born on 04 Jul 1844 in Logan, Falls Township, Hocking
     County, Ohio. He died on 13 Nov 1904 in Logan, Hocking County, Ohio. He married Almeda A.
     Main, daughter of William Main and Belinda Green on 11 Sep 1866 in Hocking County, Ohio.
     She was born on 29 Apr 1849 in Logan, Falls Township, Hocking County, Ohio. She died on 30
     Jan 1928 in Logan, Hocking County, Ohio.

     More About James William Davis:
     Military Service: Bet. Jul 1861-Jul 1865 in Company B, 31st Ohio Infantry, U.S.
     Army
     Occupation: 1870 in Falls Township, Hocking County, Ohio; Farm Laborer
     Occupation: 1880 in Falls Township, Hocking County, Ohio; Surveyor
     Occupation: 1900 in Falls Township, Hocking County, Ohio; Civil
     Engineer
     Burial: Shaw Cemetery, Hocking County, Ohio

     Notes for James William Davis:
           (from 1883 History of Hocking County)
     James William Davis, County Surveyor of Hocking County, was born
     in Falls Township, near Logan, July 4, 1844, a son of Levi and Mary
     A. (Rodman) Davis. In July, 1861, he enlisted in Company B, Thirty-
     first Ohio Infantry, to serve three years. In January, 1864, he
     veteranized and served till the close of the war, serving as Corporal
     from his last enlistment. He was in the bat-tles of Mill Springs,
     Shiloh, Hoover's Gap, Chickamauga, Stone River, Chattanooga, and
     in the campaign to Atlanta, and from there with Sherman to the sea.
     He was discharged in July, 1865, at Camp Chase, Ohio. After a
     short visit at home he went to Louisville, Ky., and remained two
     years, when he returned to Logan. His father being a civil engineer
     he also studied the science, and in 1872 was elected his father's
     successor as County

Surveyor, and has since filled that position, he having filled the
same position over thirty years. Sept. 11, 1866, Mr. Davis married
Almeda Mane, of Falls Township. They have two children---Ada
and Otto.

More About Almeda A. Main:
Living In: 1910 Logan, Hocking County, Ohio
Living In: 1920 Logan, Hocking County, Ohio
Burial: 02 Feb 1928 in Shaw Cemetery, Hocking County, Ohio

Notes for Almeda A. Main:
Name on her marriage record is spelled "Almeda Main". Father's name on her death certificate
is spelled "William Main".

James William Davis and Almeda A. Main had the following children:

    i.   Ada[3] Davis was born about 1867 in Ohio.

    ii.   Otto Davis was born about 1872 in Ohio.

    iii.   Vernon Davis was born on 15 May 1887 in Logan, Hocking County, Ohio. He died on
02 Jan 1940 in Columbus, Franklin County, Ohio. He married Nellie Doves.

More About Vernon Davis:
Occupation: 1900 in Falls Township, Hocking County, Ohio; Laborer at
Factory
Occupation: 1910 in Logan, Hocking County, Ohio; House Painter
Living In: 1910 With his mother in Logan, Hocking County, Ohio.
Burial: 04 Jan 1940 in East Lawn Cemetery

    iv.   Dottie Davis was born in Dec 1888 in Ohio. She married Lehman E. Miller
about 1909. He was born about 1889 in New York.

More About Dottie Davis:
Living In: 1910 Dottie and her husband are living with her mother in Logan,
Hocking County, Ohio.

7.   Eliza A.[2] Davis (Levi[1]) was born on 20 Nov 1846 in Logan, Hocking county, OhioOhio. She
married (1) John W. Sniff, son of Isaiah Sniff and Elizabeth Moore on 25 Dec 1866 in
Hocking County, Ohio. He was born on 13 Feb 1842 in Vinton County, Ohio. He died on 16
Jan 1904 in Falls Township, Hocking County, Ohio. She married (2) Charles Simpson, son of
Charles Simpson and Jemima Sutton on 10 Apr 1908 in Hocking County, Ohio. He was born
on 31 Mar 1853 in Pittsburgh, Allegheny County, Pennsylvania.

More About John W. Sniff:
Living In: 1870 Starr Township, Hocking County, Ohio
Living In: 1880 Falls Township, Hocking County, Ohio
Living In: 1900 Falls Township, Hocking County, Ohio
Occupation: Farmer

Notes for John W. Sniff:
Birth date is from age at death on death record.

John W. Sniff and Eliza A. Davis had the following children:

    i.   JOHN[3] SNIFF was born on 30 Nov 1867 in Falls Township, Hocking County, Ohio. He died on 09 Jul 1889 in Falls Township, Hocking county, Ohio.

More About John Sniff:
Cause Of Death: Spinal Meningitis

Notes for John Sniff:
Birth date is from age in years given on death record.

----

16.   ii. MARY ELIZABETH (FLORENCE) SNIFF was born on 09 Oct 1869 in Starr Township, Hocking County, Ohio. She died on 04 Sep 1949 in Columbus, Franklin County, Ohio. She married JOHN O. JONES. He was born on 31 Mar 1876 in Somerset, Perry County, Ohio. He died on 01 Oct 1940 in Columbus, Franklin County, Ohio. She married (2) ARTHUR H. MCLAFFERTY on 22 Jul 1888 in Point Pleasant, Mason County, West Virginia. He was born in Jul 1861 in Ohio. He died on 09 Mar 1931 in Marion Township, Franklin County, Ohio.

    iii.   LEVI T. SNIFF was born on 24 Sep 1871 in Falls Township, Hocking County, Ohio.

More About Levi T. Sniff:
Occupation: 1900 in Falls Township, Hocking County, Ohio; Farm Laborer
Living In: 1900 With his parents in Falls Township, Hocking County, Ohio

    iv.   BLANCHE SNIFF was born on 28 Mar 1874 in Falls Township, Hocking County, Ohio. She died on 30 Nov 1915 in Columbus, Franklin County, Ohio. She married Walter Ewing Carlisle, son of Harner H. Carlisle and Charlotte Griffith on 09 Jul 1899 in Greene County, Ohio. He was born on 06 Jan 1877 in Marshall Township, Highland County, Ohio. He died in Oct 1956.

More About Blanche Sniff:
Burial: 02 Dec 1915 in Green Lawn Cemetery, Columbus, Franklin County, Ohio

17.   v. MAUD LEONORRA SNIFF was born on 05 Oct 1875 in Logan, Falls Township, Hocking County, Ohio. She died on 09 Sep 1931 in Columbus, Franklin County, Ohio. She married (1) THOMAS EMERY MORSE, son of William Morse and Ida Stewart on 05 Aug 1924 in Franklin County, ohio. He was born on 26 Jun 1882 in Watertown, Jefferson County, New York. He died on 23 Jan 1945 in Columbus, Franklin County, Ohio. She married (2) ELMER E. BOWERS on 02 Apr 1893 in Hocking County, Ohio. He was born in 1868. He died on 14 Dec 1897 in Washington Township, Hocking County, Ohio. She married (3) DANIEL SMALLEY STUMP, son of Jonas Stump and Prudence Smalley on 06 Jun 1899 in Greene County, Ohio. He was born on 16 Sep 1839 in New Burlington, Greene County, Ohio. He died on 26 Nov 1925 in Spring Valley, Greene County, Ohio. She married (4) SIMON PETER WEED, son of John Weed and Louisa Goodwin on 10 Jun 1915 in Parkersburg, Wood County, West Virginia. He was born on 02 Sep 1867 in New Plymouth, Ohio. He died on 30 Aug 1932 in Columbus, Franklin County, Ohio. She married (5) GEORGE BARBER before 05 Aug 1924.

    vi.   WILLIAM LITTLETON SNIFF was born on 25 Apr 1882 in Falls Township, Hocking County, Ohio. He died on 21 Mar 1963 in Montgomery County, Ohio. He married

Ruth A. Queen, daughter of Jonas Queen and Laverna Webb on 27 Apr 1901 in Hocking County, Ohio. She was born on 10 Apr 1884 in Meigs County, Ohio.

More About William Littleton Sniff:
Living In: 1910 With his sister, Mary, and her family in Columbus, Franklin County, Ohio.

    vii.   VIOLA SNIFF was born on 31 Jan 1887 in Logan, Falls Township, Hocking County, Ohio. She died on 14 Apr 1907 in Columbus, Franklin County, Ohio. She married Orrin L. Phillips, son of Lorenzo D. Phillips and Nancy Collings on 18 Dec 1905 in Franklin County, Ohio. He was born on 17 Mar 1884 in Loveland, Ohio. He died on 31 Mar 1912 in Columbus, Franklin County, Ohio.

More About Viola Sniff:
Burial: 15 Apr 1907 in Logan, Hocking county, Ohio
Cause Of Death: Meningitis

Notes for Viola Sniff:
Given name on her death certificate is "Laura".

Generation 3

8.   **HARRIETT**[3] **DAVIS** (Levi[2], Levi[1]) was born on 05 Apr 1876 in Laurel Township, Hocking County, Ohio. She died on 20 Aug 1950 in Oakland, Alameda County, California. She married Elza Allen Doss on 26 May 1895 in Pickaway County, Ohio. He was born on 11 Feb 1873 in Crawford County, Kansas. He died on 23 Aug 1956 in Oakland, Alameda County, California.

More About Harriett Davis:
Burial: Evergreen Cemetery, Oakland, California

More About Elza Allen Doss:
Occupation: 1900 in Perry Township, Hocking County, Ohio; Farm Labor
Occupation: 1910 in Hocking Township, Fairfield County, Ohio; Working in Shoe Factory
Occupation: 1920 in Greenfield Township, Fairfield County, Ohio; Farm Laborer
Occupation: 1930 in Oakland, Alameda County, California; Receiving Clerk in Auto Factory
Occupation: 1940 in Oakland, Alameda County, California; Sweeper at Fisher Body
Burial: Evergreen Cemetery, Oakland, California

Elza Allen Doss and Harriett Davis had the following children:

    i.   WILLIAM WESLEY[4] DOSS was born on 16 Aug 1895 in Harrison Township, Pickaway County, Ohio. He died on 18 Dec 1955 in Dayton, Ohio. He married LEORA M. COVER. She was born on 24 Jan 1897. She died on 10 Sep 1963 in Lancaster, Fairfield County, Ohio.

More About William Wesley Doss:
Occupation: 1910 in Hocking Township, Fairfield County, Ohio; Helper in Glass Factory
Military Service: Bet. 22 Jul-08 Dec 1918 in World War One; Company C, 5th Development Battalion, 158th Depot Brigade
Burial: New Oakthorpe Cemetery, Oakthorpe, Fairfield County, Ohio

ii.   MARY ELLEN DOSS was born on 27 Mar 1898 in Pickaway County, Ohio. She died on 03 Feb 1992 in Butte County, California. She married William Bryan Laessle, son of William F. Laessle and Anna Borkwitz on 03 May 1924. He was born on 18 Sep 1896 in Lancaster, Fairfield County, Ohio. He died on 02 Jan 1985 in Butte County, California.

iii.   EMMETT ALLEN DOSS was born on 14 Nov 1899 in Hocking County, Ohio. He died on 02 Jun 1930.

More About Emmett Allen Doss:
Occupation: 1920 in Greenfield Township, Fairfield County, Ohio; Glass Factory Laborer
Occupation: 1930 in Oakland, Alameda County, California; Elevator Operator
Living In: 1930 With his parents in Oakland, Alameda County, California.

18.   iv.   LEE EUGENE DOSS was born on 17 Apr 1901 in Hocking County, Ohio. He died on 9 Feb 1983 in Alameda County, California. He married (1) MAUD EDITH COMPTON, daughter of Oscar Compton and Elizabeth Williams on 31 Oct 1931 in Alameda County, California. She was born on 08 Sep 1894 in Pennsylvania. She died on 31 Mar 1989 in Alameda County, California. He married LENA ETHEL SHAEFFER. She was born on 21 Oct 1906 in Hocking Township, Fairfield County, Ohio.

vi.   RALPH EDWARD DOSS was born on 07 Jan 1908 in Lancaster, Ohio. He died on 07 Mar 1992 in Carson City, Nevada. He married RUTH CLAIR HYATT. She was born on 6 Apr 1914 in California. She died on 08 Aug 1983 in Carson City, Nevada.

More About Ralph Edward Doss:
Burial: Lone Mountain Cemetery, Carson City, Nevada

19.   vi.   RUSSELL ALBERT DOSS was born on 02 Aug 1909 in Lancaster, Ohio. He died on 02 Jan 1991 in Butte County, California. He married Zena Mary McMillan, daughter of Peter McMillan and (unknown) Hildenbrand on 21 Mar 1931. She was born on 30 Jun 1912 in California. She died on 11 Aug 1982 in Butte County, California.

vii.   ELZA J. DOSS was born about 1917 in Ohio.

9.   LYCURGUS[3] DAVIS (Levi[2], Levi[1]) was born on 18 Oct 1880 in Falls Township, Hocking County, Ohio. He died on 14 Apr 1928 in Columbus, Franklin County, Ohio. He married Myrtle Chambers, daughter of Alexander Chambers and Ellen C. Lendennen on 29 Apr 1903 in Logan, Hocking County, Ohio. She was born on 23 Feb 1880 in Laurel Township, Hocking County, Ohio.

More About Lycurgus Davis:
Occupation: 1900 in Laurel Township, Hocking County, Ohio; Day Laborer
Occupation: 1910 in Lancaster, Fairfield County, Ohio; Watchman at Shoe Factory
Occupation: 1918 in Columbus, Franklin County, Ohio; Shoe worker at H.C. Godman Company
Occupation: 1920 in Columbus, Franklin County, Ohio; Laborer at Motor Company
Occupation: 1928 in Columbus, Franklin County, Ohio; Street Car Conductor
Burial: 17 Apr 1928 in Memorial Burial Park

Notes for Lycurgus Davis:
Ohio birth index gives first name as Lycusgus and birth date of November 15, 1880. Marriage Record gives birth date as October 18, 1880. World War One draft registration gives birth date as

October 18, 1880. Death certificate gives October 18, 1881 as birth date but age in years given on death certificate indicates a birth year of 1880.

Started using "Curtis" for first name at some point in time between 1910 and 1918.

More About Myrtle Chambers:
Living In: 1930 Columbus, Franklin County, Ohio
Burial: Green Lawn Cemetery, Columbus, Ohio

More About Lycurgus Davis and Myrtle Chambers:
Marriage Fact: Married by Rev. E. G. Guartney

Lycurgus Davis and Myrtle Chambers had the following children:

    i. DWIGHT D .[4] DAVIS was born on 11 Jul 1904 in Hocking County, Ohio. He died on 06 Feb 1963 in Franklin County, Ohio. He married Gazelle G. Conner, daughter of Anson L. Conner and Ollie A. Edgar on 26 Nov 1927 in Madison County, Ohio. She was born on 22 Mar 1906 in Columbus, Franklin County, Ohio.

    More About Dwight D. Davis:
    Living In: 1930 Dwight and Gazelle are living with his mother in Columbus, Franklin County, Ohio.

    ii. WAYNE CHAMBERS DAVIS was born on 02 Apr 1906 in Lancaster, Fairfield County, Ohio. He died on 07 Aug 1965 in Columbus, Ohio. He married Rose Mary Rickenbacker, daughter of John Rickenbacker and Theresa Vought on 21 Aug 1928 in Franklin County, Ohio. She was born on 09 Jul 1907 in Columbus, Franklin County, Ohio.

20.   iii. JOSAPHINE DAVIS was born on 11 Jan 1908 in Lancaster, Fairfield County, Ohio. She died in 1990. She married Claude Walters, son of Samuel F. Walters and Anna May Albright on 01 Apr 1924 in Franklin County, Ohio. He was born on 30 Dec 1904 in Gahannah, Franklin County, Ohio.

10.   **SAMUEL BIGHAM**[3] **DAVIS** (Levi[2], Levi[1]) was born on 07 Dec 1882 in Sunset, Hocking County, Ohio. He died on 19 Dec 1976 in Bucyrus, Crawford County, Ohio. He married Effie E. Gwartney, daughter of Emmet Gwartney and Margaret Williams on 30 Nov 1905 in Lancaster, Ohio. She was born on 25 Apr 1885 in Perry Township, Hocking County, Ohio. She died on 02 Feb 1961 in Columbus, Franklin County, Ohio.

More About Samuel Bigham Davis:
Occupation: 1900 in Laurel Township, Hocking County, Ohio; Day Laborer
Occupation: 1910 in Lancaster, Fairfield County, Ohio; Street Car Motorman
Occupation: 1920 in Perry Township, Hocking County, Ohio; Farmer
Occupation: 1930 in Hocking Township, Fairfield County, Ohio; Farmer
Occupation: 1940 in Hocking Township, Fairfield County, Ohio; Farmer
Living In: 1976 Fairfield County, Ohio
Burial: Amanda Township Cemetery, Amanda, Fairfield County, Ohio

More About Effie E. Gwartney:
Living In: 1961 Fairfield County, Ohio
Burial: Amanda Township Cemetery, Amanda, Fairfield County, Ohio

Samuel Bigham Davis and Effie E. Gwartney had the following children:

    i. WALTER S.[4] DAVIS was born in 1907 in Lancaster, Ohio. He died on 23 May 1970 in Gallipolis, Ohio.

        Notes for Walter S. Davis:
        Adopted before April 15, 1910.

    ii. BEULAH LEONA DAVIS was born on 25 Jun 1913 in Hocking County, Ohio. She died on 30 Jul 1999 in Bucyrus, Crawford County, Ohio. She married Pearl E. Walters, son of Edward M. Walters and Anna Huffman on 20 Nov 1941. He was born on 14 Oct 1907 in Hocking Township, Fairfield County, Ohio. He died on 14 May 1984 in Bucyrus, Crawford County, Ohio.

        More About Beulah Leona Davis:
        Burial: 03 Aug 1999 in Oakwood Cemetery, Bucyrus, Crawford County, Ohio

    iii. LLOYD RICHARD DAVIS was born on 23 Jun 1915 in Hocking County, Ohio. He died on 26 Dec 2003 in Fairfield County, Ohio. He married Helen Betty Smith on 12 Jun 1937. She was born on 05 Jul 1914 in Ohio. She died on 12 Feb 2003 in Fairfield County, Ohio.

        More About Lloyd Richard Davis:
        Living In: 2003 Amanda, Fairfield County, Ohio
        Burial: Amanda Township Cemetery, Amanda, Fairfield County, Ohio

21.   iv. MARY LEOTA DAVIS was born on 02 Sep 1918 in Hocking County, Ohio. She married Dale Frederick Metcalf on 17 Dec 1939. He was born on 16 Jul 1915 in West Union, West Virginia. He died on 10 Aug 2010 in Lancaster, Fairfield County, Ohio.

    v. MARGARET EILEEN DAVIS was born on 13 Jun 1921 in Lancaster, Fairfield County, Ohio. She married William Heimlich, son of Peter Heimlich and Mary Tustin on 13 Jun 1944 in Franklin County, Ohio. He was born on 17 May 1920 in Ashville, Pickaway County, Ohio. He died on 03 Oct 1953 in Columbus, Franklin County, Ohio.

    vi. EVA MABLE DAVIS was born on 12 May 1923 in Lancaster, Ohio. She married Charles Kinser on 22 Oct 1944. He was born on 20 Aug 1924 in Ohio.

11. **SARAH DELL[3] DAVIS** (Levi[2], Levi[1]) was born on 24 Dec 1885 in Laurel Township, Hocking County, Ohio. She died on 01 Nov 1957 in Athens, Ohio. She married Daniel Bailey, son of Charles Bailey and Christena Deischle on 28 Dec 1905 in Hocking County, Ohio. He was born on 02 Nov 1875 in Rockbridge, Good Hope Township, Hocking County, Ohio. He died on 20 Dec 1956 in Logan, Ohio.

More About Sarah Dell Davis:
Burial: Union Church Cemetery, Good Hope Township, Hocking County, Ohio

Notes for Sarah Dell Davis:
Marriage Record gives birthplace as Laurel Township, Hocking County, Ohio.

More About Daniel Bailey:
Occupation: 1900 in Good Hope Township, Hocking County, Ohio; Pipe Line Labor
Occupation: 1910 in Good Hope Township, Hocking County, Ohio; Labor on Gas Line
Occupation: 1920 in Good Hope Township, Hocking County, Ohio; Farmer
Occupation: 1930 in Good Hope Township, Hocking County, Ohio; Farm Operator
Occupation: 1940 in Good Hope Township, Hocking County, Ohio; Farmer
Burial: Union Church Cemetery, Good Hope Township, Hocking County, Ohio

Notes for Daniel Bailey:
World War One draft registration has birth date of October 2, 1875. 1900 U.S. census has birth date of November 1875. Headstone has birth year of 1875. Ohio Births has birth date of October 3, 1876.

Daniel Bailey and Sarah Dell Davis had the following children:

i. ELMER ALLEN[4] BAILEY was born on 23 Jul 1906 in Good Hope Township, Hocking County, Ohio. He died on 27 Jan 1964 in Columbus, Franklin County, Ohio. He married Nettie Lucille Carpenter, daughter of William J. Carpenter and Sarah Flowers in Jun 1938. She was born on 25 Sep 1908 in Good Hope Township, Hocking County, Ohio. She died on 15 Mar 1990 in Lancaster, Fairfield County, Ohio.

More About Elmer Allen Bailey:
Occupation: 1930 in Good Hope Township, Hocking County, Ohio; Road Foreman on State Road
Living In: 1930 With his parents in Good Hope Township, Hocking County, Ohio.
Living In: 1964 Hocking County, Ohio

ii. FLORENCE BAILEY was born on 13 Sep 1908 in Hocking County, Ohio. She died on 09 Jun 1974. She married Earl R. Brown on 09 Mar 1929. He was born on 19 Jun 1908 in Ohio. He died on 10 Jun 1981 in Lancaster, Fairfield County, Ohio.

More About Florence Bailey:
Living In: 1974 Fairfield County, Ohio

iii. GLADYS MARY BAILEY was born on 15 Oct 1910 in Hocking County, Ohio. She died on 16 Apr 1996 in Lancaster, Fairfield County, Ohio. She married James Gilbert Inboden, son of Sheldon Inboden and Zola Coakley on 01 Sep 1928 in Washington County, Ohio. He was born on 29 Apr 1909 in Ohio. He died on 14 Jul 1950 in Nelsonville, Athens County, Ohio.

More About Gladys Mary Bailey:
Burial: Union Church Cemetery, Good Hope Township, Hocking County, Ohio

iv. HARRY BAILEY was born on 20 Nov 1912 in Hocking County, Ohio. He died on 19 Mar 1918 in Rockbridge, Good Hope Township, Hocking County, Ohio.

More About Harry Bailey:
Burial: 19 Mar 1918 in Union Church Cemetery, Good Hope Township, Hocking County, Ohio
Cause Of Death: Diphtheria

v. HARVEY DAVIS BAILEY was born on 28 Sep 1915 in Hocking County, Ohio. He died on 23 Apr 1982 in Palm Beach County, Florida. He married Cora Catherine Conley on 19 Sep 1936. She was born in 1918. She died on 07 Sep 1974 in Logan, Hocking County, Ohio.

More About Harvey Davis Bailey:
Burial: Knollwood Cemetery, Logan, Hocking County, Ohio

vi. LEOTA BAILEY was born on 08 Oct 1919 in Hocking County, Ohio. She died on 20 Dec 1920 in Good Hope Township, Hocking County, Ohio.

vii. MABEL LUETTA BAILEY was born on 07 Feb 1922 in Good Hope Township, Hocking County, Ohio. She died on 02 Feb 2005 in Logan, Hocking County, Ohio. She married Willis Chambers on 13 May 1939. He was born on 19 Dec 1912 in Ohio. He died on 25 Sep 1988 in Logan, Hocking County, Ohio.

More About Mabel Luetta Bailey:
Burial: Fairview Methodist Church Cemetery, Good Hope Township, Hocking County, Ohio

viii. LOY EUGENE BAILEY was born on 02 Dec 1923 in Hocking County, Ohio. He died on 29 Jun 2002 in Logan, Hocking County, Ohio. He married Freda Hutchinson on 05 Aug 1948. She was born on 24 Jun 1926.

More About Loy Eugene Bailey:
Military Service: SSML3, U.S. Navy, World War Two
Burial: Knollwood Cemetery, Logan, Hocking County, Ohio

12. **MARY ANN**[3] **DAVIS** (Levi[2], Levi[1]) was born on 16 Mar 1887 in Laurel Township, Hocking County, Ohio. She died on 11 Mar 1971 in Lakeland, Polk County, Florida. She married William Edward Tucker, son of Hollis Clark Tucker and Clara Fox on 29 Jun 1906 in Lancaster, Ohio. He was born on 08 Nov 1885 in Rockbridge, Ohio. He died on 21 Apr 1975 in Plant City, Florida.

More About Mary Ann Davis:
Occupation: School Teacher
Burial: Pleasant Grove Cemetery, Durant, Florida

More About William Edward Tucker:
Living In: 1908 Rockbridge, Goodhope Township, Hocking County, Ohio
Living In: 1910 Good Hope Township, Hocking County, Ohio
Occupation: 1920 in Columbus, Franklin County, Ohio; Structural Iron Worker on Bridge Work
Occupation: 1930 in Columbus, Franklin County, Ohio; Iron Worker Building Bridges
Occupation: 1940 in Columbus, Franklin County, Ohio; Iron Worker with Iron Contractor
Burial: Pleasant Grove Cemetery, Durant, Florida

Notes for William Edward Tucker:
Working as a Union Iron Worker at Jackson Iron and Steel Company, Jackson, Ohio in 1942.

William Edward Tucker and Mary Ann Davis had the following children:

22. i. WILLIAM HOLLIS[4] TUCKER was born on 28 Jan 1907 in Good Hope Township, Hocking County, Ohio. He died on 13 May 1951 in Nelsonville, Ohio. He married

Mazie Ellen Turbett, daughter of Charles Monroe Turbett and Cora Bell Bartley on 02 May 1931 in Franklin County, Ohio. She was born on 10 Feb 1910 in Columbus, Franklin County, Ohio. She died on 11 Jan 1996 in Pickaway County, Ohio.

ii. EVLYN MARIE TUCKER was born on 18 Jul 1908 in Millville, Hocking County, Ohio. She died on 19 Mar 1988 in Athens, Athens County, Ohio. She married ARTHUR B. HILT. He was born on 16 May 1916 in Hocking County, Ohio. He died on 07 Jun 1963 in Nelsonville, Athens County, Ohio. She married (2) EARL CHARLES SALTZ, son of Charles Saltz and Laura Yearling on 15 Jun 1931 in Franklin County, Ohio. He was born on 15 Feb 1899 in Columbus, Franklin County, Ohio. He died on 14 May 1971 in Big Spring, Howard County, Texas.

More About Evlyn Marie Tucker:
Occupation: 1930 in Columbus, Franklin County, Ohio; Cutter in Shoe Factory
Living In: 1930 With her parents in Columbus, Franklin County, Ohio.
Military Service: Bet. 29 Aug 1944-10 Jan 1945 in Enlisted July 31, 1944 at Fort Hayes, Columbus, Ohio; U. S. Army, World War Two
Living In: 1988 Vinton County, Ohio
Burial: Pleasant Grove Cemetery, Durant, Florida

Notes for Evlyn Marie Tucker: No Children.

Enlisted in Womens Army Corps at Fort Hayes, Columbus, Ohio on July 31, 1944. Reported for active duty August 29, 1944 at Cleveland, Ohio. Service number A 512 088.

----

23. iii. PHYLLIS OLENE TUCKER was born on 21 Mar 1922 in Columbus, Ohio. She died on 7 Mar 1991 in Lancaster, Ohio. She married Robert McDaniel Stewart, son of Van Robert Stewart and Elsie Myrtle Casto on 27 Sep 1940 in Logan, Hocking County, Ohio. He was born on 17 Dec 1920 in Mason County, West Virginia. He died on 18 Jul 1977 in Plant City, Florida.

13. **ESENA BELL**[3] **DAVIS** (Levi[2], Levi[1]) was born on 05 Jun 1889 in Hocking County, Ohio. She died on 15 Jul 1982 in Columbus, Franklin County, Ohio. She married Wilmer Joseph Jackson, son of Joseph Jackson and Ida Bell on 03 Mar 1906. He was born on 14 Aug 1886 in Sugar Grove, Franklin County, Ohio. He died on 18 Sep 1969 in Columbus, Ohio.

More About Esena Bell Davis:
Burial: Forest Lawn Cemetery, Columbus Ohio

More About Wilmer Joseph Jackson:
Occupation: 1910 in Greenfield Township, Fairfield County, Ohio; Section Laborer on Railroad
Occupation: 1917 in Columbus, Franklin County, Ohio; Locomotive Fireman on Hocking Valley Railroad
Occupation: 1920 in Columbus, Franklin County, Ohio; Engineer on Hocking Valley Railroad
Occupation: 1930 in Columbus, Franklin County, Ohio; Railroad Mechanic
Occupation: 1941 in Columbus, Franklin County, Ohio; Locomotive Engineer
Occupation: 1942 in Columbus, Franklin County, Ohio; Working on C&O
Railroad Burial: Forest Lawn Cemetery, Columbus Ohio

Wilmer Joseph Jackson and Esena Bell Davis had the following children:

i.   JOSEPH LEE[4] JACKSON was born on 01 Apr 1907 in Violet Township, Fairfield County, Ohio. He died on 26 Sep 1967 in Hocking County, Ohio. He married (1) JULIA ELIZABETH ROOT in 1934. She was born on 25 Sep 1913 in Delaware County, Ohio. She died on 09 Apr 1996 in Logan, Hocking County, Ohio. He married (2) MINNIE (UNKNOWN) before 09 Apr 1930. She was born about 1912 in Ohio. He married (3) RUTH BUTLER, daughter of Clarence Butler and Illinita Furr on 04 May 1946 in Franklin County, Ohio. She was born on 17 Jul 1909 in Aurora, Illinois.

More About Joseph Lee Jackson:
Living In: 1967 Logan, Hocking County, Ohio

Notes for Joseph Lee Jackson:
Ohio County Births gives name as Joseph L. Jackson. Ruth Butler marriage record gives name as Lee J. Jackson. Ohio death index gives name as Lee J. Jackson. 1910 U.S. census has his name as Lee J. Jackson. 1920 and 1930 U.S. census has his name as Lee Jackson.

----

ii.   VIOLET MAE JACKSON was born on 15 Dec 1909 in Carroll, Fairfield County, Ohio. She died on 04 Dec 1998 in Springfield, Clark County, Ohio. She married Glenn Edwin Swartzwalder, son of Phillip P. Schwartzwalder and Lucy S. Priode on 01 Dec 1927 in Franklin County, Ohio. He was born on 16 Sep 1903 in Sutton Township, Meigs County, Ohio.

iii.   ROBERT WILMER JACKSON was born on 19 Jun 1912 in Columbus, Ohio. He died in Apr 1980. He married (UNKNOWN) JERREL. He married (2) GERALDINE FARRAND on 05 Dec 1931.

More About Robert Wilmer Jackson:
Living In: 1980 Columbus, Franklin County, Ohio

iv.   CARLITA VIRGINIA JACKSON was born on 12 Oct 1914 in Columbus, Ohio. She died on 04 Jun 1976 in Columbus, Franklin County, Ohio. She married Ishmael Blake, son of Joseph Blake and Carlita V. Jackson on 13 Aug 1930 in Franklin County, Ohio. He was born on 23 Aug 1912 in Ohio. He died on 10 Feb 1977 in Franklin County, Ohio.

More About Carlita Virginia Jackson:
Living In: 1976 Columbus, Franklin County, Ohio
Burial: Obetz Cemetery, Obetz, Franklin County, Ohio

14.   LYDA JANE[3] DAVIS (Levi[2], Levi[1]) was born on 25 Dec 1891 in Laurel Township, Hocking County, Ohio. She died on 25 Nov 1981 in Lancaster, Fairfield County, Ohio. She married Anthony Shonk, son of Arron Shonk and Catherine Wohlsheid on 15 Jul 1912. He was born on 14 Jan 1877 in Madison Township, Fairfield County, Ohio. He died on 20 Oct 1943 in Lancaster, Fairfield County, Ohio.

More About Lyda Jane Davis:
Occupation: 1910 in Madison Township, Fairfield County, Ohio; Working as a servant in the home of Anthony Shonk.
Burial: St. Mary's Cemetery, Lancaster, Fairfield County, Ohio

More About Anthony Shonk:
Occupation: 1900 in Madison Township, Fairfield County, Ohio; Farm Laborer
Living In: 1900 With his parents in Madison Township, Fairfield County, Ohio.
Occupation: 1910 in Madison Township, Fairfield County, Ohio; Farmer
Occupation: 1918 in Lancaster, Fairfield County, Ohio; Farmer
Occupation: 1920 in Madison Township, Fairfield County, Ohio; Farmer
Occupation: 1930 in Madison Township, Fairfield County, Ohio; Farmer
Occupation: 1940 in Madison Township, Fairfield County, Ohio; Farm
Operator Burial: St. Mary's Cemetery, Lancaster, Fairfield County, Ohio

Anthony Shonk and Lyda Jane Davis had the following children:

 i. RALPH F.[4] SHONK was born on 01 Oct 1913 in Fairfield County, Ohio. He died on 10 Sep 1964 in Lancaster, Fairfield County, Ohio. He married MOLLY J . CORDLE. She was born on 27 Apr 1911 in Kentucky. She died on 17 Feb 1987 in Cuyahoga Falls, Summit County, Ohio.

  More About Ralph F. Shonk:
  Burial: St. Mary's Cemetery, Lancaster, Fairfield County, Ohio

 ii. KATHRYN CECELIA SHONK was born on 04 Aug 1915 in Fairfield County, Ohio. She died on 14 Nov 2000 in Lancaster, Fairfield County, Ohio. She married BURNSIE LEVI MOORE. He was born on 28 Jun 1914 in Lawrence County, Kentucky. He died on 10 Jan 2003 in Lancaster, Fairfield County, Ohio.

  More About Kathryn Cecelia Shonk:
  Burial: Floral Hills Memory Gardens, Lancaster, Fairfield County, Ohio

 iii. RUTH M. SHONK was born on 02 May 1918 in Fairfield County, Ohio. She died on 31 May 1912 in Lancaster, Fairfield County, Ohio. She married Meryl H. Seesholtz on 19 Feb 1938. He was born on 07 Feb 1914 in Ohio. He died on 20 Mar 1984 in Lancaster, Fairfield County, Ohio.

  More About Ruth M. Shonk:
  Burial: St. Mary's Cemetery, Lancaster, Fairfield County, Ohio

 iv. HAROLD A. SHONK was born on 16 Dec 1926 in Fairfield County, Ohio. He died on 29 Apr 2007 in Ohio. He married EVELYN L. AZBELL. She was born on 19 May 1926 in Ohio. She died on 28 Nov 2010 in Ohio.

  More About Harold A. Shonk:
  Living In: 2007 Lancaster, Fairfield County, Ohio

 v. JOSEPH H. SHONK was born on 01 Jan 1929 in Fairfield County, Ohio. He died on 16 Apr 2000 in Florida. He married (UNKNOWN) THOMPSON.

  More About Joseph H. Shonk:
  Living In: 2000 Fort Lauderdale, Broward County, Florida

 vi. BETTY ELIZABETH SHONK was born on 30 Jan 1932 in Ohio. She died on 04 Apr 1989 in Zanesville, Muskingum County, Ohio. She married Joseph William Henwood, son of Charles A. Henwood and Kathleen Leftbridge on 02 Sep 1950 in

Fairfield County, Ohio. He was born on 08 Oct 1928 in Ohio. He died on 21 May 2009 in Circleville, Pickaway County, Ohio.

More About Betty Elizabeth Shonk:
Living In: 1989 Lancaster, Fairfield County, Ohio
Burial: St. Mary's Cemetery, Lancaster, Fairfield County, Ohio

15.   **NELSON B.**[3] **DAVIS** (Levi[2], Levi[1]) was born on 01 Jul 1895 in Laurel Township, Hocking County, Ohio. He died on 06 Nov 1978 in Fairfield County, Ohio. He married Helen Carrie Kane, daughter of Salem Kane and Mattie Wilson on 19 Jul 1919. She was born on 28 Aug 1901 in Hocking County, Ohio. She died on 01 May 1978 in Lancaster, Fairfield County, Ohio.

More About Nelson B. Davis:
Military Service: Bet. 30 May 1917-21 Apr 1919 in 148th Infantry, U. S. Army; World War One
Occupation: 1920 in Hocking Township, Fairfield County, Ohio; House Carpenter
Occupation: 1930 in Greenfield Township, Fairfield County, Ohio; Contract Carpenter
Occupation: 1940 in Lancaster, Fairfield County, Ohio; Building Contractor
Occupation: 1942 in Lancaster, Fairfield County, Ohio; Building Contractor
Burial: Floral Hills Memory Gardens, Lancaster, Fairfield County, Ohio

Notes for Nelson B. Davis:
Headstone has 1979 for year of death.

Served in Ypres-Lys and Meuse-Argonne sectors with the American Expeditionary Force in France during World War One.
Served in Company G, 148th Infantry until June 10, 1918. Served in Medical department 148th Infantry June 10, 1918 until discharge.

More About Helen Carrie Kane:
Burial: Floral Hills Memory Gardens, Lancaster, Fairfield County, Ohio

Nelson B. Davis and Helen Carrie Kane had the following child:

    i.   KENNETH RUSSELL[4] DAVIS was born on 01 Feb 1920 in Fairfield County, Ohio. He died on 19 Aug 2004 in Fairfield County, Ohio. He married NAOMI VAUGHAN HAWKINS. She was born on 07 May 1918 in West Virginia. She died on 21 May 2013 in Lancaster, Fairfield County, Ohio. He married (2) DOROTHY MARTIN on 12 Dec 1943. She was born on 19 Jun 1919. She died on 25 Sep 1960 in Lancaster, Fairfield County, Ohio.

        More About Kenneth Russell Davis:
        Occupation: 1940 in Lancaster, Fairfield County, Ohio; Building and Construction Carpenter
        Military Service: U.S. Army Air Corps, World War Two
        Burial: Floral Hills Memory Gardens, Lancaster, Fairfield County, Ohio

16.   **MARY ELIZABETH (FLORENCE)**[3] **SNIFF** (Eliza A.[2] Davis, Levi[1] Davis) was born on 09 Oct 1869 in Starr Township, Hocking County, Ohio. She died on 04 Sep 1949 in Columbus, Franklin County, Ohio. She married **JOHN O . JONES**. He was born on 31 Mar 1876 in Somerset, Perry County, Ohio. He died on 01 Oct 1940 in Columbus, Franklin County, Ohio. She married (2) **ARTHUR H. MCLAFFERTY** on 22 Jul 1888 in Point Pleasant, Mason County, West Virginia. He was born in Jul 1861 in Ohio. He died on 09 Mar 1931 in Marion Township, Franklin County, Ohio.

More About Mary Elizabeth (Florence) Sniff:
Living In: 1900 Xenia, Greene County, Ohio
Living In: 1910 Columbus, Franklin County, Ohio
Living In: 1920 Columbus, Franklin County, Ohio
Burial: 07 Sep 1949 in Sunset Cemetery, Columbus, Ohio

More About John O. Jones:
Burial: 04 Oct 1940 in Memorial Park, Columbus, Ohio

More About Arthur H. McLafferty:
Burial: 11 Mar 1931 in Memorial Park, Columbus, Ohio

Arthur H. McLafferty and Mary Elizabeth (Florence) Sniff had the following children:

    i.   BLANCH[4] MCLAFFERTY was born on 01 Jun 1889 in Ohio. She died on 11 May 1936 in Columbus, Franklin County, Ohio. She married LIMCOTT L. SMITH.

        More About Blanch McLafferty:
        Burial: 14 May 1936 in Memorial Burial
        Park Cause Of Death: ; Tuberculosis

    ii.   ARTHUR EUGENE MCLAFFERTY was born on 06 Jul 1892 in Spring Valley, Greene County, Ohio. He died on 03 Dec 1938 in Columbus, Franklin County, Ohio. He married Essie M. Durham, daughter of John Durham and Rhoda Fultz on 15 Feb 1920 in Franklin County, Ohio. She was born on 26 Jun 1889 in Charleston, West Virginia.

        More About Arthur Eugene McLafferty:
        Cause Of Death: Tuberculosis

17.   MAUD LEONORRA[3] SNIFF (Eliza A.[2] Davis, Levi[1] Davis) was born on 05 Oct 1875 in Logan, Falls Township, Hocking County, Ohio. She died on 09 Sep 1931 in Columbus, Franklin County, Ohio. She married (1) THOMAS EMERY MORSE, son of William Morse and Ida Stewart on 05 Aug 1924 in Franklin County, ohio. He was born on 26 Jun 1882 in Watertown, Jefferson County, New York. He died on 23 Jan 1945 in Columbus, Franklin County, Ohio. She married (2) ELMER E. BOWERS on 02 Apr 1893 in Hocking County, Ohio. He was born in 1868. He died on 14 Dec 1897 in Washington Township, Hocking County, Ohio. She married (3) DANIEL SMALLEY STUMP, son of Jonas Stump and Prudence Smalley on 06 Jun 1899 in Greene County, Ohio. He was born on 16 Sep 1839 in New Burlington, Greene County, Ohio. He died on 26 Nov 1925 in Spring Valley, Greene County, Ohio. She married (4) SIMON PETER WEED, son of John Weed and Louisa Goodwin on 10 Jun 1915 in Parkersburg, Wood County, West Virginia. He was born on 02 Sep 1867 in New Plymouth, Ohio. He died on 30 Aug 1932 in Columbus, Franklin County, Ohio. She married (5) GEORGE BARBER before 05 Aug 1924.

More About Maud Leonorra Sniff:
Living In: 1900 Spring Valley, Greene County, Ohio
Living In: 1910 Spring Valley, Greene County, Ohio
Living In: 1920 Logan, Hocking County, Ohio
Living In: 1930 Columbus, Franklin County, Ohio
Burial: 10 Sep 1931 in Memorial Park, Galloway, Franklin County, Ohio

More About Thomas Emery Morse:
Burial: 26 Jan 1945 in Wesley Chapel Cemetery

More About Elmer E. Bowers:
Cause Of Death: Gun Shot Wound
Burial: Ewing Cemetery, Ewing, Hocking County, Ohio

Elmer E. Bowers and Maud Leonorra Sniff had the following children:

i.	BERNARD HERMAN[4] BOWERS was born on 06 Mar 1894 in Washington Township, Hocking County, Ohio. He died on 25 May 1950 in Columbus, Franklin County, Ohio.

More About Bernard Herman Bowers:
Burial: 29 May 1950 in Sunset Cemetery, Columbus, Ohio

ii.	RAYMOND BOWERS was born on 10 Sep 1897 in Hocking County, Ohio. He died on 09 Mar 1962 in Columbus, Franklin County, Ohio. He married Mildred Nash, daughter of George Nash and Myrtle Smith on 06 Sep 1919. She was born on 07 May 1903 in Athens County, Ohio.

More About Daniel Smalley Stump:
Burial: 28 Nov 1925 in Spring Valley, Greene County, Ohio

More About Simon Peter Weed:
Burial: 02 Sep 1932 in Green Lawn Cemetery, Columbus, Franklin County, Ohio

Generation 4

18.	LEE EUGENE[4] DOSS (Harriett[3] Davis, Levi[2] Davis, Levi[1] Davis) was born on 17 Apr 1901 in Hocking County, Ohio. He died on 09 Feb 1983 in Alameda County, California. He married (1) **MAUD EDITH COMPTON**, daughter of Oscar Compton and Elizabeth Williams on 31 Oct 1931 in Alameda County, California. She was born on 08 Sep 1894 in Pennsylvania. She died on 31 Mar 1989 in Alameda County, California. He married **LENA ETHEL SHAEFFER**. She was born on 21 Oct 1906 in Hocking Township, Fairfield County, Ohio.

More About Lee Eugene Doss:
Occupation: 1930 in Oakland, Alameda County, California; Restaurant Cook
Living In: 1930 With his parents in Oakland, Alameda County, California.
Living In: 1940 Lee and Maud are living with his parents in Oakland, Alameda County, California.
Occupation: 1940 in Oakland, Alameda County, California; Auto Assembly at Fisher Body

More About Maud Edith Compton:
Occupation: 1940 in Oakland, Alameda County, California; Counter Girl at Commercial Cafeteria

Lee Eugene Doss and Lena Ethel Shaeffer had the following child:

i.	CLARENCE EDWARD[5] DOSS was born on 03 Oct 1923 in Fairfield County, Ohio. He died on 27 Aug 1990 in Alameda County, California.

More About Clarence Edward Doss:
Living In: 1930 With his maternal grandparents in Greenfield Township, Fairfield County, Ohio.
Living In: 1940 With his father and step mother in Oakland, Alameda County, California.

19.	RUSSELL ALBERT[4] DOSS (Harriett[3] Davis, Levi[2] Davis, Levi[1] Davis) was born on 02 Aug 1909 in Lancaster, Ohio. He died on 02 Jan 1991 in Butte County, California. He married Zena Mary

McMillan, daughter of Peter McMillan and (unknown) Hildenbrand on 21 Mar 1931. She was born on 30 Jun 1912 in California. She died on 11 Aug 1982 in Butte County, California.

Russell Albert Doss and Zena Mary McMillan had the following child:

  i. EUGENE ALBERT[5] DOSS was born on 20 Oct 1933 in Alameda County, California.

20. JOSAPHINE[4] DAVIS (Lycurgus[3], Levi[2], Levi[1]) was born on 11 Jan 1908 in Lancaster, Fairfield County, Ohio. She died in 1990. She married Claude Walters, son of Samuel F. Walters and Anna May Albright on 01 Apr 1924 in Franklin County, Ohio. He was born on 30 Dec 1904 in Gahannah, Franklin County, Ohio.

More About Josaphine Davis:
Occupation: 1930 in Columbus, Franklin County, Ohio; Stretcher at Shoe Factory

More About Claude Walters:
Occupation: 1930 in Columbus, Franklin County, Ohio; Clerk for Steam Railroad
Living In: 1930 Claude and his family are living with Josephine's mother in Columbus, Franklin County, Ohio.

Claude Walters and Josaphine Davis had the following children:

  i. CLAUDE E.[5] WALTERS was born about 1925 in Ohio.

  ii. MARY L. WALTERS was born about 1930 in Ohio.

21. MARY LEOTA[4] DAVIS (Samuel Bigham[3], Levi[2], Levi[1]) was born on 02 Sep 1918 in Hocking County, Ohio. She married Dale Frederick Metcalf on 17 Dec 1939. He was born on 16 Jul 1915 in West Union, West Virginia. He died on 10 Aug 2010 in Lancaster, Fairfield County, Ohio.

Notes for Mary Leota Davis:
Birth date might be August 2, 1918.

More About Dale Frederick Metcalf:
Burial: Floral Hills Memory Gardens, Lancaster, Fairfield County, Ohio

Notes for Dale Frederick Metcalf:
Lancaster: Dale F. Metcalf, 95, went home to be with his Lord August 9, 2010.

Born in West Union, West Virginia on July 16, 1915. Later the family moved to Lancaster, Ohio.

He was a 1935 graduate of Lancaster High School and School Colors were Purple and Gold and retired from IBEW Local 683 in 1980.

He was a charter member of the Lancaster United Brethren in Christ Church where he led various offices. He had a lot of hobbies, traveling, hunting, bowling, bicycle riding and photography. He bowled for the Thursday Senior Citizens for years. He was a member of Olivedale Senior Citizens.

Dale is survived by his wife, Mary Metcalf for 70 years; son, Kenneth (Catherine) Metcalf all of Lancaster, Ohio; grandchildren, Deborah (Mike) Clifford of Sugar Grove, Ohio, Kyle (Nicole) Metcalf and Allen Metcalf of Texas, Kary (Sue) Metcalf of Jacksonville, Florida, Kory Metcalf (Lori Kidwell friend) of Grove City, Ohio; two step-grandchildren, Kim Timmerman of North Carolina and Rod Reynolds of of Florida; seven great-grandchildren; three step-great-grandchildren; one great-great-grandson.

He was preceded in death by son, Dennis Metcalf; parents, William Anna Metcalf; six brothers, Alvin, Layman,Vernon, Trevor, William and Kenneth Metcalf; and six sisters, Opal Reese, Rhea Hulkenberg, Ruth Smith, Gilda Henderickson, Ruby and Hazel Metcalf.

Funeral services will be held 19:30 a.m. Friday at the Lancaster United Brethren Christ Church with Rev. Greg Voight and Rev. Henry Cadwell officiating.

Friends and relatives may call Thursday 2-4 & 6-8 p.m. at the Halteman-Fett & Dyer Funeral Home, Lancaster, Ohio.

Originally published in the Lancaster Eagle Gazette August 11, 2010

Dale Frederick Metcalf and Mary Leota Davis had the following child:

     i.   DENNIS^5 METCALF.

22.   **WILLIAM HOLLIS**^{4} **TUCKER** (Mary Ann^3 Davis, Levi^2 Davis, Levi^1 Davis) was born on 28 Jan 1907 in Good Hope Township, Hocking County, Ohio. He died on 13 May 1951 in Nelsonville, Ohio. He married Mazie Ellen Turbett, daughter of Charles Monroe Turbett and Cora Bell Bartley on 02 May 1931 in Franklin County, Ohio. She was born on 10 Feb 1910 in Columbus, Franklin County, Ohio. She died on 11 Jan 1996 in Pickaway County, Ohio.

More About William Hollis Tucker:
Occupation: 1930 in Columbus, Franklin County, Ohio; Iron Worker Building Bridges
Living In: 1930 With his parents in Columbus, Franklin County, Ohio.
Occupation: 1931 in Franklin County, Ohio; Painter
Burial: 16 May 1951 in Mount Olive Cemetery, South Perry, Hocking County, Ohio Military Service: Company D, 29th Engineer Battalion, U.S. Army, World War   Two
Cause Of Death: Coronary Thrombosis
Occupation: Magician

Notes for William Hollis Tucker:
Served in Company D, 29th Engineer Battalion, U.S. Army, World War Two.

More About Mazie Ellen Turbett:
Burial: Mount Olive Cemetery, South Perry, Hocking County, Ohio

William Hollis Tucker and Mazie Ellen Turbett had the following children:

     i.   HOLLIS DAVIS^5 TUCKER was born on 27 Jan 1933 in Ohio. He died on 09 May 1984 in Palm Beach County, Florida. He married ARLENE (UNKNOWN).

    ii.   CHARLES EDWARD TUCKER was born on 29 Jul 1937 in Ohio. He died on 19 Apr 1980 in Franklin County, Ohio. He married MIRIUM (UNKNOWN).

        More About Charles Edward Tucker:
        Military Service: Bet. 01 Nov 1954-25 Nov 1955 ; U.S. Air Force
        Burial: Mount Olive Cemetery, South Perry, Hocking County, Ohio

    iii.   ARTHUR LEE TUCKER was born on 24 Aug 1943 in Columbus, Ohio. He died on 27 May 2009 in Ashville, Ohio. He married BELINDA (UNKNOWN).

        More About Arthur Lee Tucker:

Military Service: United States Air Force
Cause Of Death: Lung Cancer
Burial: Mount Olive Cemetery, South Perry, Hocking County, Ohio

iv.   CAROLYN SUE TUCKER. She married DARRELL GRIFFITH.

23.   **PHYLLIS OLENE[4] TUCKER** (Mary Ann[3] Davis, Levi[2] Davis, Levi[1] Davis) was born on 21 Mar 1922 in Columbus, Ohio. She died on 07 Mar 1991 in Lancaster, Ohio. She married Robert McDaniel Stewart, son of Van Robert Stewart and Elsie Myrtle Casto on 27 Sep 1940 in Logan, Hocking County, Ohio. He was born on 17 Dec 1920 in Mason County, West Virginia. He died on 18 Jul 1977 in Plant City, Florida.

More About Phyllis Olene Tucker:
Burial: 11 Mar 1991 in New Fairview Cemetery, Logan, Ohio

More About Robert McDaniel Stewart:
Living In: 1935 Toledo, Lucas County, Ohio
Occupation: 1938 in Hocking County, Ohio; Working in Electrical Refrigeration
Occupation: Apr 1940 in Logan, Hocking County, Ohio; Cab Driver for Cab Company
Occupation: Sep 1940 in South Perry, Hocking County, Ohio; Bar Tender
Burial: 21 Jul 1977 in Pleasant Grove Cemetery, Durant, Florida

Robert McDaniel Stewart and Phyllis Olene Tucker had the following children:

i.   MARY SANDRA[5] STEWART was born on 17 Nov 1942 in Columbus, Ohio. She married HARRY DAVENPORT. She married HAROLD OATES.

ii.   EVLYN MARIE STEWART was born on 17 Dec 1944 in South Perry, Ohio. She married FRANKLIN EUGENE TIMMS. He was born on 03 May 1940 in Dundas, Ohio.

iii.   JON ROBERT STEWART was born on 15 Dec 1947 in Logan, Ohio. He died on 17 Dec 1947 in Logan, Ohio.

More About Jon Robert Stewart:
Burial: 18 Dec 1947 in Smith Chapel Cemetery, Logan, Hocking County, Ohio Cause Of Death: ; Premature

Notes for Jon Robert Stewart:
Buried with his paternal grandparents.

iv.   HOPE ELLEN STEWART was born on 27 Jun 1949 in South Perry, Ohio. She married David Garland Edwards on 09 Mar 1968 in Tampa, Florida. He was born on 21 May 1945 in Fort Sumner, New Mexico.

Descendants of William Bigham

Generation 1

1. **WILLIAM**[1] **BIGHAM** was born in 1760 in County Armagh, Ireland. He died in 1844 in Wills Township, Guernsey County, Ohio. He married **SARAH BARTON**. She was born in 1765 in Ireland. She died on 05 Oct 1826 in Wills Township, Guernsey County, Ohio.

More About William Bigham:
Burial: Old Washington Cemetery, Old Washington, Guernsey County, Ohio

More About Sarah Barton:
Burial: Old Washington Cemetery, Old Washington, Guernsey County, Ohio

William Bigham and Sarah Barton had the following children:

    i. JAMES W.[2] BIGHAM was born in 1784 in Ireland. He died in 1842 in Guernsey County, Ohio. He married Elizabeth McCreary on 26 Mar 1818.

2.   ii. SAMUEL BIGHAM was born about 1800 in County Armagh, Ireland. He died on 31 Oct 1836 in Richland Township, Guernsey County, Ohio. He married Sarah Morris, daughter of Isaac Morris and Sarah McBurney on 08 Mar 1821 in Guernsey County, Ohio. She was born on 20 Nov 1802 in Pennsylvania. She died on 30 Jun 1870 in Rockbridge, Hocking County, Ohio.

    iii. JANE BIGHAM was born on 11 Jun 1801 in Ireland. She died on 29 Sep 1865 in Wills Township, Guernsey County, Ohio. She married William B. Stewart on 09 Sep 1843 in Guernsey County, Ohio.

More About Jane Bigham:
Burial: Old Washington Cemetery, Old Washington, Guernsey County, Ohio

3.   iv. SARAH BIGHAM was born on 25 Mar 1803 in Ireland. She died on 15 Dec 1846 in Washington Township, Guernsey County, Ohio. She married James Clarke in Mar 1845 in Guernsey County, Ohio. He was born in 1796. He died in 1879.

    v. MARGARET BIGHAM was born in 1806. She married Isaac Warden on 13 Jan 1824 in Guernsey County, Ohio. He was born in 1794. He died in 1866 in Guernsey County, Ohio.

    vi. REBECCA BIGHAM was born in 1808.

    vii. WILLIAM BIGHAM was born in 1810.

Generation 2

2. **SAMUEL**[2] **BIGHAM** (William[1]) was born about 1800 in County Armagh, Ireland. He died on 31 Oct 1836 in Richland Township, Guernsey County, Ohio. He married Sarah Morris, daughter of Isaac Morris and Sarah McBurney on 08 Mar 1821 in Guernsey County, Ohio. She was born on 20 Nov 1802 in Pennsylvania. She died on 30 Jun 1870 in Rockbridge, Hocking County, Ohio.

More About Samuel Bigham:
Burial: Old Washington Cemetery, Guernsey County, Ohio
Cause Of Death: Calomel Poisoning

More About Sarah Morris:

Burial: Brown Cemetery, Goodhope Township, Hocking County, Ohio

Samuel Bigham and Sarah Morris had the following children:

4.   i.   MARGARET[3] BIGHAM was born in 1822 in Guernsey County, Ohio. She died in 1883 in Hocking County, Ohio. She married John Botts on 10 Aug 1837 in Guernsey County, Ohio. He was born about 1815 in Ohio.

5.   ii. WILLIAM BIGHAM was born on 09 Dec 1825 in Guernsey County, Ohio. He died on 6 Mar 1896 in Kaufman County, Texas. He married Hannah Calistia Julian, daughter of Stephen Julian and Hannah Berry on 10 Aug 1848 in Fairfield County, Ohio. She was born on 27 Mar 1827 in Clear Creek Township, Fairfield County, Ohio. She died on 30 Aug 1872 in Illinois.

6.   iii. ISAAC BIGHAM was born on 10 Mar 1828 in Guernsey County, Ohio. He died on 29 Nov 1896 in Laurel Township, Hocking County, Ohio. He married (1) MARY ELIZABETH DELONG, daughter of Samuel Franklin Delong and Mary Ann Kimble on 16 Apr 1850 in Hocking County, Ohio. She was born on 19 Jan 1831 in Laurel Township, Hocking County, Ohio. She died on 30 Jun 1877 in Hocking County, Ohio. He married (2) SOPHIA JULIAN, daughter of Eli Julian and Emeline Julian on 09 Apr 1879 in Hocking County, Ohio. She was born on 02 Oct 1840 in Hocking County, Ohio. She died on 06 Mar 1921 in Chico, California.

vii.   iv. ABRAHAM BIGHAM was born on 30 Oct 1830 in Guernsey County, Ohio. He died on Nov 1877 in Van Wert County, Ohio. He married Sarah Mann, daughter of James T. Mann and Caroline Worthman on 06 Feb 1851 in Hocking County, Ohio. She was born about Aug 1834 in Hocking County, Ohio. She died on 13 Feb 1884 in Van Wert County, Ohio.

3. **SARAH[2] BIGHAM** (William[1]) was born on 25 Mar 1803 in Ireland. She died on 15 Dec 1846 in Washington Township, Guernsey County, Ohio. She married James Clarke in Mar 1845 in Guernsey County, Ohio. He was born in 1796. He died in 1879.

More About Sarah Bigham:
Burial: Old Washington Cemetery, Old Washington, Guernsey County, Ohio

James Clarke and Sarah Bigham had the following child:
      i.   JAMES[3] CLARK was born in 1846.

4. **MARGARET[3] BIGHAM** (Samuel[2], William[1]) was born in 1822 in Guernsey County, Ohio. She died in 1883 in Hocking County, Ohio. She married John Botts on 10 Aug 1837 in Guernsey County, Ohio. He was born about 1815 in Ohio.

More About John Botts:
Occupation: 1850 in Good Hope Township, Hocking County, Ohio; Farmer
Occupation: 1860 in Macon County, Illinois; Farmer

John Botts and Margaret Bigham had the following children:
      i.   WILLIAM[4] BOTTS was born about 1840 in Ohio.

      ii. MARY BOTTS was born about 1842 in Ohio.

      iii. MARTHA BOTTS was born about 1844 in Ohio.

    iv.   ELIZABETH BOTTS was born about 1846 in Ohio.

    v.   HANNAH BOTTS was born about 1849 in Ohio.

    vi.   JOHN BOTTS was born about 1851 in Ohio.

    vii.   JANE BOTTS was born about 1853 in Ohio.

    viii.   ISAAC BOTTS was born about 1859 in Ohio.

5.   WILLIAM[3] BIGHAM (Samuel[2], William[1]) was born on 09 Dec 1825 in Guernsey County, Ohio. He died on 06 Mar 1896 in Kaufman County, Texas. He married Hannah Calistia Julian, daughter of Stephen Julian and Hannah Berry on 10 Aug 1848 in Fairfield County, Ohio. She was born on 27 Mar 1827 in Clear Creek Township, Fairfield County, Ohio. She died on 30 Aug 1872 in Illinois.

More About William Bigham:
Burial: Dry Creek Cemetery, Kaufman County, Texas
Occupation: 1850 in Perry Township, Hocking County, Ohio; Carpenter
Occupation: 1860 in Laurel Township, Hocking County, Ohio; Farmer
Occupation: 1870 in Flat Branch, Shelby County, Illinois; House Carpenter
Occupation: 1880 in Kaufman County, Texas; Farming

More About Hannah Calistia Julian:
Burial: Prairie Home Cemetery, Moweaqua, Shelby County, Illinois

William Bigham and Hannah Calistia Julian had the following children:

    i.   JOSHUA ROGERS[4] BIGHAM was born on 01 Oct 1852 in Laurel Township, Hocking County, Ohio. He died on 12 Nov 1942 in Mineola, Wood County, Texas. He married Elizabeth Jane Showers about 1878. She was born on 09 Dec 1859 in Pennsylvania. She died on 18 May 1928 in Wood County, Texas.

        More About Joshua Rogers Bigham:
        Burial: 12 Nov 1942 in Bigham Family Cemetery, Mineola, Wood County, Texas

    ii.   AMBROSE BIGHAM was born in Jan 1856 in Laurel Township, Hocking County, Ohio. He died in May 1912 in Ardmore, Carter County, Oklahoma. He married Daltha T. Graham about 1898. She was born about 1878 in Tennessee. She died after 23 Apr 1910 in Texas.

        More About Ambrose Bigham:
        Occupation: Farmer
        Occupation: Postmaster in Tona, Texas

        Notes for Ambrose Bigham:
        From the "Daily Ardmoreite" published in Ardmore, Carter County, Oklahoma on 26 Jan 1912:

        "Destitute Family Must Have Help".

        "Neighbors of A. W. Bigham who resides on B Street Southwest reported to the Ardmoreite this morning that Mr. Bigham and his family are in dire need, very sick and is not expected to live. His wife died sometime ago. He has seven children, the oldest of whom is but 12 years of age, and the baby is seriously ill with pneumonia. Something must be done or the family will perish...

"Later: the remains of A. W. Bigham were laid to rest in Rose Hill cemetery. Rev. C. Raymond Gray of the Broadway Methodist church conducted the services. The children were left without money, without home and without parents. Mrs. James H. Mathers took 3 of the children, Miss Pearl Moore cared for another. Suggested Cornish Orphans Home..
"Later in March, Probation officer Mrs. Curtis has placed the Bigham children in good homes and she is delighted with the manner in which are they being cared for. It had been hoped that the twins would get in the same home and not be separated, but such could not be done, however, the twins are in the same family and will be associated together. Mrs. Curtiss has written a history of the case, giving the age and name of each child and the person who has taken each child and placed this history in the care of each child so that in later years they may be able to locate one another.".

----

  iii. EMMA MELICIA BIGHAM was born on 30 Oct 1858 in Laurel Township, Hocking County, Ohio. She died on 27 Nov 1893 in Kaufman County, Texas.

    More About Emma Melicia Bigham:
    Burial: Dry Creek Cemetery, Kaufman County, Texas

8. iv. SARAH FELICCA BIGHAM was born on 22 Dec 1861 in Butler County, Ohio. She died on 29 Apr 1939 in Kaufman County, Texas. She married James Daniel Coates, son of James Coates and Artelia Francis walker on 10 Nov 1886 in Kaufman County, Texas. He was born on 08 Oct 1864 in Kentucky. He died on 13 Aug 1934 in Van Zandt County, Texas.

  v. ELIZABETH BARBRIA BIGHAM was born on 07 May 1867 in Flat Branch, Shelby County, Illinois. She died on 10 Aug 1893 in Kaufman County, Texas.

    More About Elizabeth Barbria Bigham:
    Burial: Dry Creek Cemetery, Kaufman County, Texas

6. **ISAAC**[3] **BIGHAM** (Samuel[2], William[1]) was born on 10 Mar 1828 in Guernsey County, Ohio. He died on 29 Nov 1896 in Laurel Township, Hocking County, Ohio. He married (1) **MARY ELIZABETH DELONG**, daughter of Samuel Franklin Delong and Mary Ann Kimble on 16 Apr 1850 in Hocking County, Ohio. She was born on 19 Jan 1831 in Laurel Township, Hocking County, Ohio. She died on 30 Jun 1877 in Hocking County, Ohio. He married (2) **SOPHIA JULIAN**, daughter of Eli Julian and Emeline Julian on 09 Apr 1879 in Hocking County, Ohio. She was born on 02 Oct 1840 in Hocking County, Ohio. She died on 06 Mar 1921 in Chico, California.

More About Isaac Bigham:
Burial: Brown Cemetery, Good Hope Township, Hocking County, Ohio
Occupation: 1850 in Good Hope Township, Hocking County, Ohio; Farmer
Occupation: 1860 in Laurel Township, Hocking County, Ohio; Farmer
Occupation: 1870 in Laurel Township, Hocking County, Ohio; Farmer
Occupation: 1880 in Laurel Township, Hocking County, Ohio; Farmer

More About Mary Elizabeth Delong:
Burial: Betheny Church Cemetery, Hocking County, Ohio

Isaac Bigham and Mary Elizabeth Delong had the following children:

i.   ABRAHAM[4] BIGHAM was born on 03 Jul 1849 in Hocking County, Ohio. He died on 02 May 1931 in Perry Township, Hocking County, Ohio. He married (1) MARGARET BYERS, daughter of John S. Byers and Nancy Eaton on 13 Oct 1870 in Hocking County, Ohio. He married (2) SEENITH CROY on 22 Sep 1877 in Hocking County, Ohio. She was born in May 1853 in Ohio. He married (3) MATILDA MCGRADY, daughter of Unknown and Ellen McGrady on 15 Apr 1914. She was born on 29 Jan 1869 in Hocking County, Ohio. She died on 25 Nov 1941 in Perry Township, Hocking County, Ohio.

More About Abraham Bigham:
Burial: 04 May 1931 in Pisgah Church Cemetery, Hocking County, Ohio Cause Of Death: Cardiac Insufficiency
Occupation: Farmer

9.   ii. SAMUEL BIGHAM was born on 11 Oct 1851 in Hocking County, Ohio. He died on 16 Jan 1922 in Lancaster, Fairfield County, Ohio. He married Charlotte E. Teeter, daughter of Curtis W. Teeter and Mary Essford on 16 Sep 1871 in Hocking County, Ohio. She was born on 27 Oct 1848 in Newark, Licking County, Ohio. She died on 24 Apr 1910 in Lancaster, Fairfield County, Ohio.

10.   iii. WILLIAM BIGHAM was born on 09 Jan 1852 in Hocking County, Ohio. He died on 15 Jun 1918 in Pleasant Township, Fairfield County, Ohio. He married Rebecca Ann Croy, daughter of Samuel Croy and Eliza Bobo on 25 Oct 1875 in Hocking County, Ohio. She was born on 06 Apr 1854 in Athens, Ohio. She died on 06 May 1945 in Logan, Ohio.

11.   iv. MARY ANN BIGHAM was born on 15 Feb 1855 in Hocking County, Ohio. She died on Aug 1924 in Greenfield Township, Fairfield County, Ohio. She married (1) LEVI DAVIS, son of Levi Davis and Mary Ann Rodman on 10 Mar 1875 in Hocking County, Ohio. He was born on 11 May 1839 in Muskingum County, ohio. He died on 08 Apr 1909 in Perry Township, Hocking County, Ohio. She married (2) NATHANIEL P. SPRINGER, son of John Springer between 08 Apr 1909-04 May 1910. He was born on 24 May 1827 in Perry County, Ohio. He died on 28 Oct 1922 in Perry Township, Hocking County, Ohio. She married (3) WILLIAM WALTON, son of Boaz Walton and Margaret Burress on 27 Sep 1923 in Franklin County, Ohio. He was born on 17 Aug 1844 in New Philadelphia, Tuscarawas County, Ohio. He died on 19 Feb 1930 in Benton Township, Hocking County, Ohio.

12.   v. SARAH BIGHAM was born on 18 Oct 1856 in Hocking County, Ohio. She died on 30 Apr 1926 in Washington Township, Hocking County, Ohio. She married (1) DANIEL NIXON on 27 Oct 1887 in Hocking County, Ohio. He was born on 13 Nov 1825 in Ohio. He died on 09 Nov 1907 in Athens County, Ohio. She married (2) JAMES FOX, son of James Fox and Nancy Clutter on 23 Jan 1873 in Hocking County, Ohio. He was born on 11 Oct 1851 in Hocking County, Ohio. He died on 14 Jul 1884 in Laurel Township, Hocking County, Ohio.

vi.   ELIZA BIGHAM was born about 1858 in Hocking County, Ohio. She died after 01 Jun 1870.

Notes for Eliza Bigham: Died young.

vii.   BYRON BIGHAM was born about Mar 1860 in Hocking County, Ohio. He died before 1 Jun 1870.

13.   viii.   ISAAC WESLEY BIGHAM was born on 26 Apr 1861 in Hocking County, Ohio. He died on 01 Feb 1923 in Perry Township, Hocking County, Ohio. He married Zelda Clapper, daughter of Jacob Clapper and Savilla Bowman on 11 Aug 1881 in Hocking County, Ohio. She was born on 05 Feb 1858 in Hocking County, Ohio. She died on 03 Nov 1922 in Perry Township, Hocking County, Ohio.

14.   ix.   JACOB BIGHAM was born on 03 Nov 1862 in Hocking County, Ohio. He died on 20 Aug 1928 in Laurel, Hocking County, Ohio. He married Rachel Deborah Seesholtz, daughter of Henry G. Seesholtz and Catherine Ebert on 14 Feb 1883 in Hocking County, Ohio. She was born on 11 Nov 1863 in South Perry, Hocking County, Ohio. She died on 24 Oct 1951 in Sugar Grove, Fairfield County, Ohio.

15.   x.   JOSEPH BIGHAM was born on 11 May 1863 in Hocking County, Ohio. He died on 24 Jul 1895 in Perry Township, Hocking County, Ohio. He married Louisa Anna Hendrickson, daughter of George Hendrickson and Mary Leisure on 03 Apr 1886 in Hocking County, Ohio. She was born on 12 Apr 1867 in Hocking County, Ohio. She died on 14 Jan 1899 in Perry Township, Hocking County, Ohio.

xi.   NELSON IGNACIUS BIGHAM was born on 09 Feb 1866 in Hocking County, Ohio. He died on 14 Dec 1936 in Laurel Township, Hocking County, Ohio. He married Eliza Jane Friend, daughter of Lorenzo Corbin Friend and Hannah Elizabeth Odell on 17 Apr 1888 in Hocking County, Ohio. She was born on 11 Sep 1868 in Hocking County, Ohio. She died on 02 May 1933 in Laurel Township, Hocking County, Ohio.

More About Nelson Ignacius Bigham:
Burial: 17 Dec 1936 in Fairview Methodist Church Cemetery, Good Hope Township, Hocking County, Ohio
Cause Of Death: Heart Disease
Occupation: Farmer

xii.   NANCY MARGARET BIGHAM was born on 09 Feb 1867 in Laurel Township, Hocking County, Ohio. She died on 24 Sep 1870 in Laurel Townshiop, Hocking County, Ohio.

More About Nancy Margaret Bigham:
Burial: Betheny Church Cemetery, Hocking County, Ohio
Cause Of Death: Burned to Death

16.   xiii.   ELIZABETH DELLA BIGHAM was born on 11 Mar 1870 in Hocking County, Ohio. She died on 23 Aug 1952 in Rockbridge, Hocking County, Ohio. She married (1) OLIVER BENWAY on 27 Oct 1884 in Central Lake, Antrim County, Michigan. He was born on Dec 1861 in Canada. He died on 24 Jul 1895 in Good Hope Township, Hocking County, Ohio. She married (2) ANDREW MARTIN ROOP, son of Martin Roop and Elizabeth Springer on 22 Apr 1897 in Hocking County, Ohio. He was born on 19 Mar 1869 in Good Hope Township, Hocking County, Ohio. He died on 22 Nov 1950 in Rockbridge, Hocking County, Ohio.

More About Sophia Julian:
Living In: 1910 With her son, Charles, and his family in Fairmount Precinct, Benton County, Oregon.

Living In: 1920 With her son, Charles, and his family in Fairmount Precinct, Benton County, Oregon.

Isaac Bigham and Sophia Julian had the following children:

xiv.　CHARLES BIGHAM was born on 30 Aug 1879 in Laurel Township, Hocking County, Ohio. He died on 14 Jan 1926 in Chico, Butte County, California. He married Elva Agnes Lizer, daughter of Lizer and Hartman on 24 Dec 1907. She was born on 07 Nov 1879 in Illinois. She died on 15 Oct 1949 in Chico, Butte County, California.

More About Charles Bigham:
Burial: Chico Cemetery, Chico, Butte County, California
Occupation: 1910 in Fairmount Precinct, Benton County, Oregon; Farmer
Occupation: 1920 in Fairmount Precinct, Benton County, Oregon; Farmer

xv.　ELI BIGHAM was born on 27 Feb 1883 in Laurel Township, Hocking County, Ohio. He died on 02 Apr 1956 in Hocking County, Ohio. He married Stella Almeda Stewart, daughter of Samuel Stewart and Emmeline Levan on 01 Jun 1912 in Lancaster, Ohio. She was born on 10 Jan 1883 in Amanda Township, Fairfield County, Ohio. She died on 06 Aug 1979 in Westerville, Franklin County, Ohio.

More About Eli Bigham:
Living In: 1910 With his brother, Charles, and his family in Fairmount Precinct, Benton County, Oregon.
Occupation: 1910 in Fairmount Precinct, Benton County, Oregon; Farmer

7.　**ABRAHAM**[3] **BIGHAM** (Samuel[2], William[1]) was born on 30 Oct 1830 in Guernsey County, Ohio. He died on 11 Nov 1877 in Van Wert County, Ohio. He married Sarah Mann, daughter of James T. Mann and Caroline Worthman on 06 Feb 1851 in Hocking County, Ohio. She was born about Aug 1834 in Hocking County, Ohio. She died on 13 Feb 1884 in Van Wert County, Ohio.

More About Abraham Bigham:
Living In: 1850 With John Wittner and his family in Good Hope Township, Hocking County, Ohio.
Occupation: 1860 in Perry Township, Hocking County, Ohio; Farmer

More About Sarah Mann:
Living In: 1880 Next door to her parents in Washington Township, Van Wert County, Ohio.

Notes for Sarah Mann:
Age at death on death record is 49 years and 6 months.

Abraham Bigham and Sarah Mann had the following children:

i.　SARAH CAROLINE[4] BIGHAM was born about 1852 in Ohio.

ii.　JOHN WESLEY BIGHAM was born about 1856 in Ohio.

iii.　JOSEPH H. BIGHAM was born about 1859 in Ohio.

iv.　MARY B. BIGHAM was born about 1870 in Ohio.

Generation 4

8.   SARAH FELICCA[4] BIGHAM (William[3], Samuel[2], William[1]) was born on 22 Dec 1861 in Butler County, Ohio. She died on 29 Apr 1939 in Kaufman County, Texas. She married James Daniel Coates, son of James Coates and Artelia Francis walker on 10 Nov 1886 in Kaufman County, Texas. He was born on 08 Oct 1864 in Kentucky. He died on 13 Aug 1934 in Van Zandt County, Texas.

More About Sarah Felicca Bigham:
Burial: 30 Apr 1939 in Locust Grove Cemetery, Hiram, Kaufman County, Texas

More About James Daniel Coates:
Burial: 14 Aug 1934 in Locust Grove Cemetery, Hiram, Kaufman County, Texas

Notes for James Daniel Coates:
Birth date is from age at death on death certificate.

James Daniel Coates and Sarah Felicca Bigham had the following children:

  i. MYRTLE GRACIE[5] COATES was born on 09 Jan 1888 in Terrell, Texas. She died on 22 Sep 1919 in Kaufman County, Texas. She married Andrew Johnson on 11 Jul 1906 in Wills Point, Texas. He was born on 22 Oct 1888 in Claiborne County, tennessee. He died on 26 Dec 1971 in Fort collins, Colorado.

  ii. JAMES DANIEL COATES was born on 13 Jul 1890 in Terrell, Texas. He died on 10 Jan 1964 in Kaufman County, Texas.

9.   SAMUEL[4] BIGHAM (Isaac[3], Samuel[2], William[1]) was born on 11 Oct 1851 in Hocking County, Ohio. He died on 16 Jan 1922 in Lancaster, Fairfield County, Ohio. He married Charlotte E. Teeter, daughter of Curtis W. Teeter and Mary Essford on 16 Sep 1871 in Hocking County, Ohio. She was born on 27 Oct 1848 in Newark, Licking County, Ohio. She died on 24 Apr 1910 in Lancaster, Fairfield County, Ohio.

More About Samuel Bigham:
Burial: 19 Jan 1922 in Brown Cemetery, Goodhope Township, Hocking County, Ohio
Cause Of Death: Chronic Myocarditis
Occupation: Farmer

More About Charlotte E. Teeter:
Burial: 26 Apr 1910 in Brown Cemetery, Goodhope Township, Hocking County, Ohio

Samuel Bigham and Charlotte E. Teeter had the following children:

  i. ETTA V.[5] BIGHAM was born in Apr 1875 in Ohio.

  ii. NOAH E. BIGHAM was born on 06 Dec 1876.

  iii. HANNAH M. BIGHAM was born in Jul 1879 in Ohio.

  iv. CHESTER BIGHAM was born in Dec 1880 in Ohio.

  v. WILLIAM B. BIGHAM was born in Dec 1882 in Ohio.

  vi. LAURA M. BIGHAM was born in May 1889 in Ohio.

10.   WILLIAM[4] BIGHAM (Isaac[3], Samuel[2], William[1]) was born on 09 Jan 1852 in Hocking County, Ohio.

He died on 15 Jun 1918 in Pleasant Township, Fairfield County, Ohio. He married Rebecca Ann Croy, daughter of Samuel Croy and Eliza Bobo on 25 Oct 1875 in Hocking County, Ohio. She was born on 06 Apr 1854 in Athens, Ohio. She died on 06 May 1945 in Logan, Ohio.

More About William Bigham:
Burial: 17 Jun 1918 in Betheny Church Cemetery, Hocking County, Ohio
Cause Of Death: Aortic Stenosis
Occupation: Farmer

William Bigham and Rebecca Ann Croy had the following children:

    i.   MARGARET[5] BIGHAM was born on 11 Apr 1876.

    ii.   ROSA LEE BIGHAM was born on 24 Jun 1887 in Dallas, Texas. She died on 16 Mar 1938 in Lancaster, Fairfield County, Ohio. She married GEORGE MASON. He died after 16 Mar 1938.

        More About Rosa Lee Bigham:
        Burial: 19 Mar 1938 in Elmwood Cemetery
        Cause Of Death: Carcinoma of Cervix

11.   MARY ANN[4] BIGHAM (Isaac[3], Samuel[2], William[1]) was born on 15 Feb 1855 in Hocking County, Ohio. She died on 07 Aug 1924 in Greenfield Township, Fairfield County, Ohio. She married (1) LEVI DAVIS, son of Levi Davis and Mary Ann Rodman on 10 Mar 1875 in Hocking County, Ohio. He was born on 11 May 1839 in Muskingum County, ohio. He died on 08 Apr 1909 in Perry Township, Hocking County, Ohio. She married (2) NATHANIEL P. SPRINGER, son of John Springer between 08 Apr 1909-04 May 1910. He was born on 24 May 1827 in Perry County, Ohio. He died on 28 Oct 1922 in Perry Township, Hocking County, Ohio. She married (3) WILLIAM WALTON, son of Boaz Walton and Margaret Burress on 27 Sep 1923 in Franklin County, Ohio. He was born on 17 Aug 1844 in New Philadelphia, Tuscarawas County, Ohio. He died on 19 Feb 1930 in Benton Township, Hocking County, Ohio.

More About Mary Ann Bigham:
Burial: 10 Aug 1924 in Pisgah Church Cemetery, Hocking County,
Ohio Cause Of Death: Addisons Disease
Living In: 1924 Lancaster, Fairfield County, Ohio

More About Levi Davis:
Burial: 10 Apr 1909 in Pisqah Church Cemetery, Hocking County,
Ohio
Cause Of Death: Bronchial Pneumonia
Living In: 1860 Levi and Mary are living next door to his father in Falls Township, Hocking County, Ohio.
Living In: 1870 Levi and Mary are living next door to her brother, David Shultz, in Hopewell Township, Muskingum County, Ohio.
Occupation: 1860 in Falls Township, Hocking County, Ohio; Farmer
Occupation: 1870 in Hopewell Township, Muskingum County, Ohio; Works on Farm
Occupation: 1880 in Falls Township, Hocking County, Ohio; Minister
Occupation: 1900 in Laurel Township, Hocking County, Ohio; Farmer
Military Service: Bet. 02 Jul 1861-02 May 1862 ; Company C. 26th Ohio Infantry, U.S. Army

Levi Davis and Mary Ann Bigham had the following children:

    i.   LEVI[5] DAVIS was born on 16 Nov 1875 in Falls Township, Hocking County, Ohio. He died on 13 May 1961 in Hocking County, Ohio. He married Emma Louise Springer, daughter of Edward Springer and Caroline Bailey on 29 Dec 1901 in Hocking County, Ohio. She was born on 25 Feb 1882 in Hocking County, Ohio. She died on

26 Jan 1982 in Circleville, Pickaway County, Ohio.

More About Levi Davis:
Burial: Pisgah Church Cemetery, Hocking County, Ohio
Living In: 1900 With his parents in Laurel Township, Hocking County, Ohio.
Occupation: 1900 in Laurel Township, Hocking County, Ohio; Day Laborer
Occupation: 1901 in Rockbridge, Hocking County, Ohio; Saw Mill Hand
Occupation: 1910 in Perry Township, Hocking County, Ohio; Farmer
Occupation: 1920 in Laurel Township, Hocking County, Ohio; Farmer
Occupation: 1930 in Laurel Township, Hocking County, Ohio; Farmer
Occupation: 1940 in Laurel Township, Hocking County, Ohio; Farmer

Notes for Levi Davis:
Never had children.

Birth record has birth date of November 30, 1875. Marriage license has birth
darte of November 16, 1875. World War One draft registration has birth date of
November 16, 1875.

    ii.   HARRIETT DAVIS was born on 05 Apr 1876 in Laurel Township, Hocking County,
Ohio. She died on 20 Aug 1950 in Oakland, Alameda County, California. She
married Elza Allen Doss on 26 May 1895 in Pickaway County, Ohio. He was
born on 11 Feb 1873 in Crawford County, Kansas. He died on 23 Aug 1956 in
Oakland, Alameda County, California.

More About Harriett Davis:
Burial: Evergreen Cemetery, Oakland, California

    iii.   ISAAC WESLEY DAVIS was born on 12 Jan 1879 in Logan, Ohio. He died on 22
Sep 1900.

More About Isaac Wesley Davis:
Burial: Pisgah Church Cemetery, Hocking County, Ohio
Occupation: 1900 in Laurel Township, Hocking County, Ohio; Day Laborer

    iv.   LYCURGUS DAVIS was born on 18 Oct 1880 in Falls Township, Hocking County,
Ohio. He died on 14 Apr 1928 in Columbus, Franklin County, Ohio. He married
Myrtle Chambers, daughter of Alexander Chambers and Ellen C. Lendennen on
29 Apr 1903 in Logan, Hocking County, Ohio. She was born on 23 Feb 1880 in
Laurel Township, Hocking County, Ohio.

More About Lycurgus Davis:
Burial: 17 Apr 1928 in Memorial Burial Park
Occupation: 1900 in Laurel Township, Hocking County, Ohio; Day Laborer
Occupation: 1910 in Lancaster, Fairfield County, Ohio; Watchman at Shoe
Factory
Occupation: 1918 in Columbus, Franklin County, Ohio; Shoeworker at H.C.
Godman Company
Occupation: 1920 in Columbus, Franklin County, Ohio; Laborer at Motor Company
Occupation: 1928 in Columbus, Franklin County, Ohio; Street Car Conductor

Notes for Lycurgus Davis:
Ohio birth index gives first name as Lycusgus and birth date of November 15, 1880. Marriage Record gives birth date as October 18, 1880. World War One draft registration gives birth date as October 18, 1880. Death certificate gives October 18, 1881 as birth date but age in years given on death certificate indicates a birth year of 1880.

Started using "Curtis" for first name at some point in time between 1910 and 1918.

----

v. SAMUEL BIGHAM DAVIS was born on 07 Dec 1882 in Sunset, Hocking County, Ohio. He died on 19 Dec 1976 in Bucyrus, Crawford County, Ohio. He married Effie E. Gwartney, daughter of Emmet Gwartney and Margaret Williams on 30 Nov 1905 in Lancaster, Ohio. She was born on 25 Apr 1885 in Perry Township, Hocking County, Ohio. She died on 02 Feb 1961 in Columbus, Franklin County, Ohio.

More About Samuel Bigham Davis:
Burial: Amanda Township Cemetery, Amanda, Fairfield County, Ohio Living In: 1976 Fairfield County, Ohio
Occupation: 1900 in Laurel Township, Hocking County, Ohio; Day Laborer
Occupation: 1910 in Lancaster, Fairfield County, Ohio; Street Car Motorman
Occupation: 1920 in Perry Township, Hocking County, Ohio; Farmer
Occupation: 1930 in Hocking Township, Fairfield County, Ohio; Farmer
Occupation: 1940 in Hocking Township, Fairfield County, Ohio; Farmer

vi. GEORGE H. DAVIS was born in Apr 1884 in Hocking County, Ohio.

More About George H. Davis:
Occupation: 1900 in Laurel Township, Hocking County, Ohio; Farm Laborer

vii. SARAH DELL DAVIS was born on 24 Dec 1885 in Laurel Township, Hocking County, Ohio. She died on 01 Nov 1957 in Athens, Ohio. She married Daniel Bailey, son of Charles Bailey and Christena Deischle on 28 Dec 1905 in Hocking County, Ohio. He was born on 02 Nov 1875 in Rockbridge, Good Hope Township, Hocking County, Ohio. He died on 20 Dec 1956 in Logan, Ohio.

More About Sarah Dell Davis:
Burial: Union Church Cemetery, Good Hope Township, Hocking County, Ohio

Notes for Sarah Dell Davis:
Marriage Record gives birthplace as Laurel Township, Hocking County, Ohio.

----

viii. MARY ANN DAVIS was born on 16 Mar 1887 in Laurel Township, Hocking County, Ohio. She died on 11 Mar 1971 in Lakeland, Polk County, Florida. She married William Edward Tucker, son of Hollis Clark Tucker and Clara Fox on 29 Jun 1906 in Lancaster, Ohio. He was born on 08 Nov 1885 in Rockbridge, Ohio. He died on 21 Apr 1975 in Plant City, Florida.

More About Mary Ann Davis:
Burial: Pleasant Grove Cemetery, Durant, Florida

Occupation: ; School Teacher

ix.   ESENA BELL DAVIS was born on 05 Jun 1889 in Hocking County, Ohio. She died on 15 Jul 1982 in Columbus, Franklin County, Ohio. She married Wilmer Joseph Jackson, son of Joseph Jackson and Ida Bell on 03 Mar 1906. He was born on 14 Aug 1886 in Sugar Grove, Franklin County, Ohio. He died on 18 Sep 1969 in Columbus, Ohio.

More About Esena Bell Davis:
Burial: Forest Lawn Cemetery, Columbus Ohio

10   CHARLES DAVIS was born on 10 Jan 1891 in Laurel Township, Hocking County, Ohio. He died on 15 Jan 1891.

More About Charles Davis:
Burial: Pisgah Church Cemetery, Hocking County, Ohio

Notes for Charles Davis:
Cemetery survey gives birth date of December 5, 1890 and death date of December 10, 1890. Birth record shows birth date of January 10, 1891.
----

11   LYDA JANE DAVIS was born on 25 Dec 1891 in Laurel Township, Hocking County, Ohio. She died on 25 Nov 1981 in Lancaster, Fairfield County, Ohio. She married Anthony Shonk, son of Arron Shonk and Catherine Wohlsheid on 15 Jul 1912. He was born on 14 Jan 1877 in Madison Township, Fairfield County, Ohio. He died on 20 Oct 1943 in Lancaster, Fairfield County, Ohio.

More About Lyda Jane Davis:
Burial: St. Mary's Cemetery, Lancaster, Fairfield County, Ohio
Occupation: 1910 in Madison Township, Fairfield County, Ohio; Working as a servant in the home of Anthony Shonk.

xii.   MINNIE DAVIS was born on 03 Oct 1893 in Hocking County, Ohio. She died on 08 Aug 1894 in Hocking County, Ohio.

More About Minnie Davis:
Burial: Pisgah Church Cemetery, Hocking County, Ohio

xiii.   NELSON B. DAVIS was born on 01 Jul 1895 in Laurel Township, Hocking County, Ohio. He died on 06 Nov 1978 in Fairfield County, Ohio. He married Helen Carrie Kane, daughter of Salem Kane and Mattie Wilson on 19 Jul 1919. She was born on 28 Aug 1901 in Hocking County, Ohio. She died on 01 May 1978 in Lancaster, Fairfield County, Ohio.

More About Nelson B. Davis:
Burial: Floral Hills Memory Gardens, Lancaster, Fairfield County, Ohio
Occupation: 1920 in Hocking Township, Fairfield County, Ohio; House Carpenter
Occupation: 1930 in Greenfield Township, Fairfield County, Ohio; Contract Carpenter

Occupation: 1940 in Lancaster, Fairfield County, Ohio; Building Contractor
Occupation: 1942 in Lancaster, Fairfield County, Ohio; Building Contractor
Military Service: Bet. 30 May 1917-21 Apr 1919 in 148th Infantry, U. S. Army;
World War One

Notes for Nelson B. Davis: Headstone
has 1979 for year of death.

Served in Ypres-Lys and Meuse-Argonne sectors with the American
Expeditionary Force in France during World War One.
Served in Company G, 148th Infantry until June 10, 1918. Served in
Medical department 148th Infantry June 10, 1918 until discharge.

More About Nathaniel P. Springer:
Burial: 30 Oct 1922 in Pisgah Church Cemetery, Hocking County, Ohio
Living In: 1920 Perry Township, Hocking County, Ohio
Occupation: 1910 in Perry Township, Hocking County, Ohio; Farmer

More About William Walton:
Burial: 21 Feb 1930 in Chestnut Grove Cemetery, Vinton County, Ohio

Notes for William Walton:
Marriage license gives birth date of august 17, 1844. Headstone has birth date of 1844.
Death certificate has birth date of September 15, 1843.

12.   SARAH[4] BIGHAM (Isaac[3], Samuel[2], William[1]) was born on 18 Oct 1856 in Hocking County, Ohio.
She died on 30 Apr 1926 in Washington Township, Hocking County, Ohio. She married (1)
DANIEL NIXON on 27 Oct 1887 in Hocking County, Ohio. He was born on 13 Nov 1825 in Ohio.
He died on 09 Nov 1907 in Athens County, Ohio. She married (2) JAMES FOX, son of James Fox
and Nancy Clutter on 23 Jan 1873 in Hocking County, Ohio. He was born on 11 Oct 1851 in
Hocking County, Ohio. He died on 14 Jul 1884 in Laurel Township, Hocking County, Ohio.

More About Sarah Bigham:
Burial: 03 May 1926 in Ewing Cemetery, Ewing, Hocking County, Ohio

More About Daniel Nixon:
Burial: Scott Creek Cemetery, Hocking County, Ohio

More About James Fox:
Burial: Brown Cemetery, Good Hope Township, Hocking County, Ohio
Cause Of Death: Consumption

Notes for James Fox:
Birth date is from age at death on head stone.

James Fox and Sarah Bigham had the following child:

      i.   HULDA M.[5] FOX was born on 09 Aug 1875.

13.   ISAAC WESLEY[4] BIGHAM (Isaac[3], Samuel[2], William[1]) was born on 26 Apr 1861 in Hocking County,
Ohio. He died on 01 Feb 1923 in Perry Township, Hocking County, Ohio. He married Zelda

Clapper, daughter of Jacob Clapper and Savilla Bowman on 11 Aug 1881 in Hocking County, Ohio. She was born on 05 Feb 1858 in Hocking County, Ohio. She died on 03 Nov 1922 in Perry Township, Hocking County, Ohio.

More About Isaac Wesley Bigham:
Burial: 04 Feb 1923 in Pisgah Church Cemetery, Hocking County, Ohio
Cause Of Death: ; Organic Heart Trouble
Occupation: Farmer

More About Zelda Clapper:
Burial: 05 Nov 1922 in Pisgah Cemetery, Good Hope Township, Hocking County, Ohio

Notes for Zelda Clapper:
Headstone has February 5, 1858 for date of birth. Death certificate has December 25, 1857 for date of birth.

Isaac Wesley Bigham and Zelda Clapper had the following children:

    i.   JAMES[5] BIGHAM was born on 06 Jul 1882.

    ii.   HENRY H. BIGHAM was born on 03 Sep 1884 in Hocking County, Ohio. He died on 03 Oct 1940 in Lancaster, Ohio. He married Margaret Lena Waters on 01 May 1904 in Fairfield County, Ohio. She was born on 04 Jun 1887 in Fairfield County, Ohio. She died on 04 Dec 1950 in Lancaster, Ohio.

        More About Henry H. Bigham:
        Burial: Pisgah Church Cemetery, Hocking County, Ohio

    3   JOHN WESLEY BIGHAM was born on 01 Dec 1886 in Hocking County, Ohio. He died in 1941.

        More About John Wesley Bigham:
        Burial: Pisgah Church Cemetery, Hocking County, Ohio

    4   EDWARD BIGHAM was born on 02 Apr 1889.

    5   BERTHA BIGHAM was born on 07 Jul 1891.

    6   MARY BIGHAM was born on 05 Oct 1893.

    7   ETHEL BIGHAM was born on 02 Apr 1896.

14.   JACOB[4] BIGHAM (Isaac[3], Samuel[2], William[1]) was born on 03 Nov 1862 in Hocking County, Ohio. He died on 20 Aug 1928 in Laurel, Hocking County, Ohio. He married Rachel Deborah Seesholtz, daughter of Henry G. Seesholtz and Catherine Ebert on 14 Feb 1883 in Hocking County, Ohio. She was born on 11 Nov 1863 in South Perry, Hocking County, Ohio. She died on 24 Oct 1951 in Sugar Grove, Fairfield County, Ohio.

More About Jacob Bigham:
Burial: 22 Aug 1928 in Forest Rose Cemetery, Lancaster, Fairfield County, Ohio

Cause Of Death: Septicemia
Occupation: Farmer

More About Rachel Deborah Seesholtz:
Burial: 27 Oct 1951 in Forest Rose Cemetery, Lancaster, Fairfield County, Ohio

Jacob Bigham and Rachel Deborah Seesholtz had the following children:

i. VILLA M AE[5] BIGHAM was born on 15 Jul 1883 in Hocking County, Ohio. She died on 18 Aug 1933.

LILLIE BELL BIGHAM was born on 27 Sep 1884 in Hocking County, Ohio. She married Levi N. Huber, son of Paul Huber and Melissa Yaules on 30 Sep 1906 in Hocking County, Ohio. He was born in 1882 in Amanda, Ohio.

JENNIE DORA BIGHAM was born on 28 Feb 1886 in Hocking County, Ohio. She died on 23 Jan 1962.

HULDA VESTA BIGHAM was born on 17 Sep 1887 in Hocking County, Ohio.

DANIEL OSCAR BIGHAM was born on 27 Oct 1889 in Hocking County, Ohio. He married Fannie Glaze, daughter of Henderson Glaze and Joanna Zeigler on 14 Sep 1914 in Hocking County, Ohio. She was born about 1890.

ALVA FERIDAN BIGHAM was born on 15 Nov 1891 in Hocking County, Ohio.

MAUDE ELIZABETH BIGHAM was born on 29 Sep 1894 in Hocking County, Ohio. She died on 10 Mar 1965.

ADA BETHEL BIGHAM was born on 14 Jan 1896 in Hocking County, Ohio.

HARVEY EDISON BIGHAM was born on 17 Jul 1897 in Hocking County, Ohio. He died on 23 Feb 1960.

FLETTA VENITIA BIGHAM was born on 28 Nov 1899 in Hocking County, Ohio. She died on 06 Jul 1901 in Hocking County, Ohio.

More About Fletta Venitia Bigham:
Burial: Pisgah Church Cemetery, Hocking County, Ohio

15. JOSEPH[4] BIGHAM (Isaac[3], Samuel[2], William[1]) was born on 11 May 1863 in Hocking County, Ohio. He died on 24 Jul 1895 in Perry Township, Hocking County, Ohio. He married Louisa Anna Hendrickson, daughter of George Hendrickson and Mary Leisure on 03 Apr 1886 in Hocking County, Ohio. She was born on 12 Apr 1867 in Hocking County, Ohio. She died on 14 Jan 1899 in Perry Township, Hocking County, Ohio.

More About Joseph Bigham:
Burial: Pisgah Church Cemetery, Good Hope Township, Hocking County, Ohio

Notes for Joseph Bigham:
Headstone has 1896 for year of death.

Bigham and Benway

by Konrad Stump, contributing writer to The Logan Daily News.

In each of our family histories, there are stories we have heard that stick with us, a lot of the time because they involve something that isn't quite explained or understood. Sometimes they are mentioned in passing, and sometimes the stories are known but there are elements that have been told incorrectly. The descendants of Joseph Bigham and Oliver Benway may know something of the story of their deaths, but we'd all like an account of the stories that have been passed down in pieces.

It was Wednesday, July 24, 1895. It was about 9 a.m. At his home in the northwestern part of Laurel Township, near Cantwell Cliffs, Joseph Bigham had been digging a well. He was preparing to build a new house, having made the excavation for the cellar and starting work on this well. He was being assisted but his brother-in-law, Oliver Benway. The evening before, they fired a blast in the well in order to get fire to burn in it, but it didn't do any good. They left the house about seven o'clock on Wednesday morning to work on the well. Joseph went down in the well, but was overcome by carbonic acid gas, which at the time was commonly called well damp. He called to Oliver to pull him up, but was too affected by the gas to hold the rope. Oliver called out for help. Mary Yantes, who was staying with the Bighams at the time, and Joseph's wife Anna, came to assist. Oliver lowered himself into the well, fanning Joseph for a few minutes in an attempt to revive him, but soon felt himself being overcome by the gas. He called for the women to pull him up; they were able to get him up about 16 to 17 feet, but he was so overcome by the gas he fell back to the bottom of the well, which at the time was about 35 feet deep.

Mary ran to the nearest neighbors about a half-mile away, and a group of men came back with her to assist. Dan Kline went down in the well to retrieve the men, but only got about half way before the gas overcame him and he needed to be pulled out. They pumped air into the well by means of a windmill and sheet, and a burning sheaf of wheat was lowered into it. Dan went back down in the bucket, tied a rope around the bodies of Joseph and Oliver, and brought them up. They had been dead for some time, it having been over an hour since Oliver first called for help. Oliver's head was badly cut from when he'd fallen back into the well.

The funerals took place at Mt. Pisgah, with the Rev. Mather officiating. Mather's sermon was delivered outside, as the people who'd come to attend the funerals couldn't fit in the church. People who were there guessed the attendees numbered around one thousand.

Here is what I can tell you of their lives. Joseph was born on May 11, 1863, in Hocking County to Isaac and Mary (Delong) Bigham. He grew up in Laurel Township, and his father worked as a farmer. On Apr 3, 1886, he married Louisa Anna Hendrickson, daughter of George and Mary (Leisure) Hendrickson. Together they had four children: Samuel Edison, Metta (who died as an infant), Alvah Medred, and Goldie Theresa. Joseph's wife, Anna, remarried to Samuel Lutz on Oct. 6, 1898, and the children surely lived with them along with Samuel's daughter from a previous marriage. However, on Jan. 14, 1899, Anna passed away. Though we can't be sure of a reason, Joseph and Anna's children were spread out by the 1900 federal census. Samuel went to live with Anna's brother, Frank. Alvah went to live with Salem and Samantha Shoemaker, and worked as a servant. Goldie went to live with two of Anna's sisters, Mary and Lavina.

Oliver Benway was born in Canada on Dec. 20, 1861. By 1880, he was living in Antrim County, Michigan, with his brother William. Their father had passed away, but their mother, Louisa, was living with them. On Oct. 27, 1884, Oliver married Elizabeth Della Bigham in Michigan. According to his obituary, Louisa lost her life in a fire not long after his marriage, and Oliver and Elizabeth moved back to Hocking County. The time of this can gauged by the births of Oliver and Elizabeth's children. They had four daughters together: Lydia, Lauretta, Minnie, and Nettie. Minnie was born in Michigan in 1892, and Nettie was born in Good Hope Township in 1894, making the move probably in 1893 or early 1894. After Oliver's death, Elizabeth remarried to Andrew Roop, on Apr. 22, 1897, in Hocking County. Andrew adopted Elizabeth's four daughters, and he and Elizabeth had four sons of their own. The last of these sons was named Oliver.

More About Louisa Anna Hendrickson:
Burial: Pisgah Church Cemetery, Good Hope Township, Hocking County,
Ohio Cause Of Death: Hemorrhage of Lungs

Notes for Louisa Anna Hendrickson:
Buried beside her first husband, Joseph Bigham.

Birth date is from age at death on her death record.

Joseph Bigham and Louisa Anna Hendrickson had the following children:

     i.   SAMUEL EDISON[5] BIGHAM.

     ii.   ALVA MELVIN BIGHAM.

     iii.   GOLDIE THERESA BIGHAM.

16.   **ELIZABETH DELLA**[4] **BIGHAM** (Isaac[3], Samuel[2], William[1]) was born on 11 Mar 1870 in Hocking County, Ohio. She died on 23 Aug 1952 in Rockbridge, Hocking County, Ohio. She married (1) **OLIVER BENWAY** on 27 Oct 1884 in Central Lake, Antrim County, Michigan. He was born on 27 Dec 1861 in Canada. He died on 24 Jul 1895 in Good Hope Township, Hocking County, Ohio. She married (2) **ANDREW MARTIN ROOP**, son of Martin Roop and Elizabeth Springer on 22 Apr 1897 in Hocking County, Ohio. He was born on 19 Mar 1869 in Good Hope Township, Hocking County, Ohio. He died on 22 Nov 1950 in Rockbridge, Hocking County, Ohio.

More About Elizabeth Della Bigham:
Burial: 26 Aug 1952 in Fairview Memorial Gardens, Rockbridge, Hocking County,
Ohio Cause Of Death: Cerebral Hemorrhage

Notes for Oliver Benway:
Marriage record states he was born in New York.

Bigham and Benway
by Konrad Stump, contributing writer to The Logan Daily News.

In each of our family histories, there are stories we have heard that stick with us, a lot of the time because they involve something that isn't quite explained or understood. Sometimes they are mentioned in passing, and sometimes the stories are known but there are elements that have been told incorrectly. The descendants of Joseph Bigham and Oliver Benway may know something of the story of their deaths, but we'd all like an account of the stories that have been passed down in pieces.

It was Wednesday, July 24, 1895. It was about 9 a.m. At his home in the northwestern part of Laurel Township, near Cantwell Cliffs, Joseph Bigham had been digging a well. He was preparing to build a new house, having made the excavation for the cellar and starting work on this well. He was being assisted but his brother-in-law, Oliver Benway. The evening before, they fired a blast in the well in order to get fire to burn in it, but it didn't do any good. They left the house about seven o'clock on Wednesday morning to work on the well. Joseph went down in the well, but was overcome by carbonic acid gas, which at the time was commonly called well damp. He called to Oliver to pull him up, but was too affected by the gas to hold the rope. Oliver called out for help. Mary Yantes, who was staying with the Bighams at the time, and Joseph's wife Anna, came to assist. Oliver lowered himself into the well, fanning Joseph for a few minutes in an attempt to revive him, but soon felt himself being overcome by the gas. He called for the women to pull him up; they were able to get him up about 16 to 17 feet, but he was so overcome by the gas he fell back to the bottom of the well, which at the time was about 35 feet deep.

Mary ran to the nearest neighbors about a half-mile away, and a group of men came back with her to assist. Dan Kline went down in the well to retrieve the men, but only got about half way before the gas overcame him and he needed to be pulled out. They pumped air into the well by means of a windmill and sheet, and a burning sheaf of wheat was lowered into it. Dan went back down in the bucket, tied a rope around the bodies of Joseph and Oliver, and brought them up. They had been dead for some time, it having been over an hour since Oliver first called for help. Oliver's head was badly cut from when he'd fallen back into the well.

The funerals took place at Mt. Pisgah, with the Rev. Mather officiating. Mather's sermon was delivered outside, as the people who'd come to attend the funerals couldn't fit in the church. People who were there guessed the attendees numbered around one thousand.

Here is what I can tell you of their lives. Joseph was born on May 11, 1863, in Hocking County to Isaac and Mary (Delong) Bigham. He grew up in Laurel Township, and his father worked as a farmer. On Apr 3, 1886, he married Louisa Anna Hendrickson, daughter of George and Mary (Leisure) Hendrickson. Together they had four children: Samuel Edison, Metta (who died as an infant), Alvah Medred, and Goldie Theresa. Joseph's wife, Anna, remarried to Samuel Lutz on Oct. 6, 1898, and the children surely lived with them along with Samuel's daughter from a previous marriage. However, on Jan. 14, 1899, Anna passed away. Though we can't be sure of a reason, Joseph and Anna's children were spread out by the 1900 federal census. Samuel went to live with Anna's brother, Frank. Alvah went to live with Salem and Samantha Shoemaker, and worked as a servant. Goldie went to live with two of Anna's sisters, Mary and Lavina.

Oliver Benway was born in Canada on Dec. 20, 1861. By 1880, he was living in Antrim County, Michigan, with his brother William. Their father had passed away, but their mother, Louisa, was living with them. On Oct. 27, 1884, Oliver married Elizabeth Della Bigham in Michigan. According to his obituary, Louisa lost her life in a fire not long after his marriage, and Oliver and Elizabeth moved back to Hocking County. The time of this can gauged by the births of Oliver and Elizabeth's children. They had four daughters together: Lydia, Lauretta, Minnie, and Nettie. Minnie was born in Michigan in 1892, and Nettie was born in Good Hope Township in 1894, making the move probably in 1893 or early 1894. After Oliver's death, Elizabeth remarried to Andrew Roop, on Apr. 22, 1897, in Hocking County. Andrew adopted Elizabeth's four daughters, and he and Elizabeth had four sons of their own. The last of these sons was named Oliver.

Oliver Benway and Elizabeth Della Bigham had the following children:

    i.   LYDIA D.[5] BENWAY was born on 16 Sep 1885 in Central Lake, Antrim County, Michigan. She died on 13 Aug 1930 in Hocking County, Ohio.

    ii.   LAURETTA ETTA BENWAY was born on 29 May 1889 in Central Lake, Antrim County, Michigan. She died on 25 Dec 1976.

    iii.   MINNIE AGNES BENWAY was born on 19 Sep 1892 in Crystal Lake, Benzie County,

Michigan. She died on 29 Nov 1943.

4.   NETTIE H. BENWAY was born on 14 Aug 1894 in Good Hope Township, Hocking County, Ohio.

More About Andrew Martin Roop:
Burial: 25 Nov 1950 in Fairview Memorial Gardens, Rockbridge, Hocking County, Ohio

Andrew Martin Roop and Elizabeth Della Bigham had the following children:

i.   MARTIN^5 ROOP was born in 1898.

ii.   OLIVER ROOP.

Notes:

Descendants of John Fox

Generation 1

1. JOHN[1] Fox was born in Dec 1780 in Pennsylvania. He died on 28 Feb 1856 in Hocking County, Ohio. He married Nancy Julien on 01 Apr 1806 in Fairfield County, Ohio. She was born on 21 Apr 1782 in Pennsylvania.

    More About John Fox:
    Burial: Mount Olive Cemetery, South Perry, Hocking County,
    Ohio Cause Of Death: Murdered by Elias Primmer

    John Fox and Nancy Julien had the following children:

    i. JAMES[2] Fox was born on 06 Jun 1811 in Hocking County, Ohio. He died on 31 Mar 1887 in Laurel Township, Hocking County, Ohio. He married NANCY CLUTTER. She was born on 17 Jun 1817 in West Virginia. She died on 30 Jan 1898 in Laurel Township, Hocking County, Ohio.

    ii. PETER FOX was born on 06 Jan 1814 in Laurel Township, Hocking County, Ohio. He died on 08 Feb 1890 in Hocking County, Ohio. He married Deborah White, daughter of James White on 04 Mar 1838 in Perry County, Ohio. She was born on 14 Feb 1817 in Hocking County, Ohio. She died on 16 Jan 1900 in Hocking County, Ohio.

    Iii WILLIAM FOX..

Generation 2

2. JAMES[2] FOX (John[1]) was born on 06 Jun 1811 in Hocking County, Ohio. He died on 31 Mar 1887 in Laurel Township, Hocking County, Ohio. He married NANCY CLUTTER. She was born on 17 Jun 1817 in West Virginia. She died on 30 Jan 1898 in Laurel Township, Hocking County, Ohio.

    More About James Fox:
    Burial: Brown Cemetery, Goodhope Township, Hocking County, Ohio

    Notes for James Fox:
    Date of birth is from age at death on headstone.

    Death record has March 31, 1887 for date of death. Headstone has March 30, 1887 for date of death.

    More About Nancy Clutter:
    Burial: Brown Cemetery, Goodhope Township, Hocking County, Ohio

    Notes for Nancy Clutter:
    Death record has January 30, 1898 for date of death. Headstone has January 31, 1898 for date of death.

    James Fox and Nancy Clutter had the following child:

    4. i. JAMES[3] Fox was born on 11 Oct 1851 in Hocking County, Ohio. He died on 14 Jul 1884 in Laurel Township, Hocking County, Ohio. He married Sarah Bigham, daughter of Isaac Bigham and Mary Elizabeth Delong on 23 Jan 1873 in Hocking County, Ohio. She was born on 18 Oct 1856 in Hocking County, Ohio. She died on

30 Apr 1926 in Washington Township, Hocking County, Ohio.

3.   PETER[2] FOX (John[1]) was born on 06 Jan 1814 in Laurel Township, Hocking County, Ohio. He died on 08 Feb 1890 in Hocking County, Ohio. He married Deborah White, daughter of James White on 04 Mar 1838 in Perry County, Ohio. She was born on 14 Feb 1817 in Hocking County, Ohio. She died on 16 Jan 1900 in Hocking County, Ohio.

More About Peter Fox:
Burial: Mount Olive Cemetery, South Perry, Hocking County, Ohio
Occupation: Bet. 1840-1880 in Laurel Township, Hocking County, Ohio; Farmer
Property: 1870 in Laurel Township, Hocking County, Ohio; 70 Acres Improved and 40 Acres Unimproved

More About Deborah White:
Burial: Mount Olive Cemetery, South Perry, Hocking County, Ohio

Peter Fox and Deborah White had the following children:

   i.   NANCY[3] FOX was born on 07 Jan 1839 in Ohio. She died on 07 Jul 1925 in Laurelville, Hocking County, Ohio. She married Jacob B. Riason, son of Reason Riason and Annie Brown on 06 Jan 1860 in Hocking County, Ohio. He was born on 17 Apr 1838 in Ohio. He died on 25 May 1916 in Laurelville, Hocking, Ohio, USA.

        More About Nancy Fox:
        Burial: 09 Jul 1925 in Green Summit Cemetery, Adelphi, Ross County, Ohio

   ii. JACOB FOX was born about 1841 in Ohio.

   iii. MARY FOX was born on 07 Nov 1842 in Laurel Township, Hocking County, Ohio. She died on 07 Sep 1932 in Perry Township, Hocking County, Ohio. She married Alfred Stump, son of Samuel E. Stump and Mary Cave on 01 Mar 1868 in Hocking County, Ohio. He was born on 04 Nov 1845 in Ohio. He died on 24 Oct 1930 in Perry Township, Hocking County, Ohio.

        More About Mary Fox:
        Burial: 09 Sep 1932 in Morgan Chapel Cemetery, Hocking County, Ohio

   iv. MARTHA FOX was born about 1845 in Ohio.

   v.   MATILDA FOX was born on 30 Mar 1847 in Ohio. She died on 30 Jan 1929 in Salt Creek Township, Pickaway County, Ohio. She married Simon Judy, son of Simon Judy and Ann Shearer on 07 Sep 1865 in Hocking County, Ohio. He was born on 12 Feb 1841 in Fairfield County, (now Hocking County), Ohio. He died on 07 Apr 1931 in Clearcreek Township, Fairfield County, Ohio.

        More About Matilda Fox:
        Burial: 01 Feb 1929 in Tarlton Cemetery, Tarlton, Pickaway County, Ohio
        Living In: 1929 Laurelville, Hocking County, Ohio

   6.   ELIZABETH FOX was born about 1849 in Ohio. She died between 08 Jun 1880-23 Mar 1885 in Ohio. She married Nelson Hedges, son of Charles Hedges and Sarah (unknown) on 03 Oct 1867 in Hocking County, Ohio. He was born on 06 Jul 1846 in Ohio. He died on 12 Dec 1916 in Perry Township, Hocking County, Ohio.

7.   SARAH FOX was born on 08 Jul 1853 in Hocking County, Ohio. She died on 11 Nov 1926 in Delaware, Delaware County, Ohio. She married Stephan Rizer, son of Henry Rizer and Martha Mauler on 13 May 1869 in Hocking County, Ohio. He was born on 13 Jul 1848 in Athens County, Ohio. He died on 03 Mar 1924 in Westerville, Franklin County, Ohio.

More About Sarah Fox:
Burial: 14 Nov 1926 in Westerville, Ohio
Living In: 1926 Columbus, Franklin County, Ohio

8.   ELLEN FOX was born on 30 Mar 1855 in Ohio. She died on 29 Mar 1918 in Salt Creek Township, Pickaway County, Ohio. She married Daniel Fetherolf, son of Daniel Fetherolf and Rebecca (unknown) on 01 Dec 1875 in Hocking County, Ohio. He was born on 20 Oct 1850 in Hocking County, Ohio. He died on 29 Mar 1947 in Circleville, Pickaway County, Ohio.

More About Ellen Fox:
Burial: 01 Apr 1918 in Prarieview Cemetery, Whisler, Pickaway County, Ohio

5.   ix. CLARA FOX was born on 27 Sep 1857 in Laurel Township, Hocking County, Ohio. She died on 30 Dec 1923 in Laurelville, Hocking County, Ohio. She married (1) HOLLIS CLARK TUCKER, son of Wesley Summers Tucker and Phebe Hutson on 16 Feb 1879 in Hocking County, Ohio. He was born on 15 Aug 1858 in Hocking County, Ohio. He died on 25 Apr 1916 in Columbus, Franklin County, Ohio. She married (2) WILLIAM COOK, son of John Cook and Nancy Price about 1875. He was born on 16 Sep 1857 in Green Township, Hocking County, Ohio. He died on 25 Apr 1919 in West Salem Township, Mercer County, Pennsylvania. She married (3) AARON STAHR on 16 Mar 1893 in Hocking County, Ohio. He was born on 21 Jun 1867 in Germany. He died on 14 May 1950 in Eaton, Preble County, Ohio.

Generation 3

4.   **JAMES**[3] **Fox** (James[2], John[1]) was born on 11 Oct 1851 in Hocking County, Ohio. He died on 14 Jul 1884 in Laurel Township, Hocking County, Ohio. He married Sarah Bigham, daughter of Isaac Bigham and Mary Elizabeth Delong on 23 Jan 1873 in Hocking County, Ohio. She was born on 18 Oct 1856 in Hocking County, Ohio. She died on 30 Apr 1926 in Washington Township, Hocking County, Ohio.

More About James Fox:
Burial: Brown Cemetery, Good Hope Township, Hocking County, Ohio Cause Of Death: Consumption

Notes for James Fox:
Birth date is from age at death on head stone.

More About Sarah Bigham:
Burial: 03 May 1926 in Ewing Cemetery, Ewing, Hocking County, Ohio

James Fox and Sarah Bigham had the following child:
      i.   HULDA M.[4] Fox was born on 09 Aug 1875.

5.   **CLARA**[3] **FOX** (Peter[2], John[1]) was born on 27 Sep 1857 in Laurel Township, Hocking County, Ohio. She died on 30 Dec 1923 in Laurelville, Hocking County, Ohio. She married (1) **HOLLIS CLARK TUCKER**, son of Wesley Summers Tucker and Phebe Hutson on 16 Feb 1879 in Hocking County, Ohio. He was born on 15 Aug 1858 in Hocking County, Ohio. He died on 25 Apr 1916 in Columbus, Franklin County, Ohio. She married (2) **WILLIAM COOK**, son of John Cook and Nancy Price about 1875. He was born on 16 Sep 1857 in Green Township, Hocking County, Ohio. He died on 25 Apr 1919 in West Salem Township, Mercer County, Pennsylvania. She married (3) **AARON STAHR** on 16 Mar 1893 in Hocking County, Ohio. He was born on 21 Jun 1867 in Germany. He died on 14 May 1950 in Eaton, Preble County, Ohio.

More About Clara Fox:
Burial: 01 Jan 1924 in Mount Olive Cemetery, South Perry, Hocking County, Ohio Cause Of Death: Bronchial Pneumonia

Notes for Clara Fox:
1860 U.S. census has Clarissa for her first name. Her sister, Sarah, had a daughter named Clarissa.

More About Hollis Clark Tucker:
Burial: 28 Apr 1916 in Fairview Methodist Church Cemetery, Good Hope Township, Hocking County, Ohio
Cause Of Death: Punctured lung from fractured ribs due to being run down by a railroad train.
Occupation: 1870; Farm Worker, Laurel, Ohio
Occupation: 1900 in Rockbridge, Goodhope Township, Hocking County, Ohio; Derrick Builder
Occupation: 1910 in Goodhope Township, Hocking County, Ohio; Laborer
Occupation: Carpenter

Notes for Hollis Clark Tucker:
Death certificate gives birth date as August 15, 1854. Age given on death certificate would give a birth date of August 15, 1858. 1900 U.S. census gives birthdate as August 1858. Hollis Tucker and Clara Fox marriage license indicates an 1858 birth.

Hollis Clark Tucker and Clara Fox had the following children:

    i.   **CHARLES JOSEPH**[4] **TUCKER** was born on 12 Oct 1879 in Hocking County, Ohio. He died on 13 Jan 1967 in Hocking County, Ohio. He married Beatrice Applegate, daughter of Walter Applegate and Miranda McFarland about 1903. She was born on 08 Mar 1883 in Lancaster, Ohio. She died on 13 Feb 1952 in Hocking County, Ohio.

       More About Charles Joseph Tucker:
       Living In: 1900 Living with his paternal grandparents in Rockbridge, Goodhope Township, Hocking County, Ohio
       Living In: 1910 Goodhope Township, Hocking County, Ohio
       Living In: 1920 Franklin, Franklin County, Ohio
       Living In: 1930 Columbus, Franklin County, Ohio
       Living In: 1940 Columbus, Franklin County, Ohio
       Occupation: 1900 in Rockbridge, Good Hope Township, Hocking County, Ohio; Rig Builder

    ii.   MARY LOVETTA TUCKER was born on 17 Aug 1883 in Perry Township, Hocking County, Ohio. She died on 17 Feb 1951 in Salt Creek Township, Hocking County, Ohio. She married William Elmer Woltz, son of Moses H. Woltz and Anna L.

Shellhammer on 14 Dec 1901 in Logan, Ohio. He was born on 30 Dec 1880 in Good Hope Township, Hocking County, Ohio. He died in 1955.

More About Mary Lovetta Tucker:
Burial: 20 Feb 1951 in Mount Olive Cemetery, South Perry, Hocking County, Ohio Cause Of Death: Coronary Thrombosis

Notes for Mary Lovetta Tucker:
Ohio Marriage Records give Rockbridge, Ohio as birthplace of Mary Tucker.

3   WILLIAM EDWARD TUCKER was born on 08 Nov 1885 in Rockbridge, Ohio. He died on 21 Apr 1975 in Plant City, Florida. He married Mary Ann Davis, daughter of Levi Davis and Mary Ann Bigham on 29 Jun 1906 in Lancaster, Ohio. She was born on 16 Mar 1887 in Laurel Township, Hocking County, Ohio. She died on 11 Mar 1971 in Lakeland, Polk County, Florida.

More About William Edward Tucker:
Burial: Pleasant Grove Cemetery, Durant, Florida
Living In: 1908 Rockbridge, Goodhope Township, Hocking County, Ohio
Living In: 1910 Good Hope Township, Hocking County, Ohio
Occupation: 1920 in Columbus, Franklin County, Ohio; Structural Iron Worker on Bridge Work
Occupation: 1930 in Columbus, Franklin County, Ohio; Iron Worker Building Bridges
Occupation: 1940 in Columbus, Franklin County, Ohio; Iron Worker with Iron Contractor

Notes for William Edward Tucker:
Working as a Union Iron Worker at Jackson Iron and Steel Company, Jackson, Ohio in 1942.

iv.   HARRY HERBERT TUCKER was born on 30 Oct 1887 in Good Hope Township, Hocking County, Ohio. He died on 10 Dec 1949 in Kansas. He married STELLA MAY (UNKNOWN). She was born on 20 Dec 1892 in Kansas. She died on 23 May 1980.

More About Harry Herbert Tucker:
Burial: Elim Lutheran Cemetery, Marquette, McPherson County, Kansas
Living In: 1917 Kansas City, Missouri
Living In: 1935 Denver, Denver County, Colorado
Living In: 1940 Marquette, McPherson County, Kansas
Occupation: 1917 in Oiler at Interstate Ice Company in Kansas City, Kansas
Occupation: 1920 in Denver, Denver County, Colorado; Machinist in Garage
Occupation: 1930 in Denver, Denver County, Colorado; Commercial Traveler for Farm Implements

More About William Cook:
Burial: 27 Apr 1919 in Kinsman Cemetery, Kinsman, Trumbull County, Ohio

William Cook and Clara Fox had the following child:
i. DELLA M.[4] COOK was born on 26 Aug 1876 in Laurel Township, Hocking county, Ohio. She died on 15 May 1900. She married William Robert Tobin, son of John

Tobin and Mariah (unknown) on 18 Mar 1893 in Hocking County, Ohio. He was born on 25 Jun 1862 in Ohio. He died on 14 Dec 1920 in Columbus, Franklin County, Ohio.

More About Della M. Cook:
Burial: Olive Cemetery, South Perry, Hocking County, Ohio
Living In: 1880 With her maternal grandparents in Laurel Township, Hocking County, Ohio.

Notes for Della M. Cook:
Clara used her birth name, "Clara Fox", as informant when she reported Della's birth.

More About Aaron Stahr:
Burial: 17 May 1950 in Mount Olive Cemetery, South Perry, Hocking County, Ohio
Cause Of Death: Cerebral Hemorrhage
Living In: 1940 With his son, Lewis, and his family in Lanier Township, Preble County, Ohio.
Occupation: 1900 in Laurel Township, Hocking County, Ohio; Farmer
Occupation: 1910 in Laurel Township, Hocking County, Ohio; Farmer
Occupation: 1920 in Laurel Township, Hocking County, Ohio; Teamster
Occupation: 1930 in Laurelville, Hocking County, Ohio; Odd Jobs Laborer
Occupation: 1940 in Lanier Township, Preble County, Ohio; Farmer

Aaron Stahr and Clara Fox had the following children:

    i.   LEWIS IRL[4] STAHR was born on 15 Feb 1896 in Gibisonville, Hocking County, Ohio. He died on 02 May 1970 in Dayton, Montgomery County, Ohio. He married Frances F. Harpold on 30 Sep 1926 in Ripley, Jackson County, West Virginia. She was born on 20 Feb 1904 in Jackson County, West Virginia. She died on 14 Apr 1987 in St. Marys, Auglaize County, Ohio.

        More About Lewis Irl Stahr:
        Burial: Mound Hill Cemetery, Eaton, Preble County, Ohio
        Living In: 1920 With his parents in Laurel Township, Hocking county, Ohio.
        Living In: 1970 in Eaton, Preble County, Ohio
        Occupation: 1920 in Laurel Township, Hocking County, Ohio; Laborer
        Occupation: 1930 in Eaton, Preble County, Ohio; Road Building Laborer
        Occupation: 1940 in Lanier Township, Preble County, Ohio; Foreman W.P.A. Road Work
        Military Service: Enlisted May 31, 1918 for World War One

        Notes for Lewis Irl Stahr:
        Social Security death index has May 15, 1970 as date of death. Ohio death index has May 2, 1970 as date of death.

    ii.   DARL STAHR was born on 28 Feb 1894 in Gibisonville, Hocking County, Ohio. He died on 15 Dec 1947 in Laurel Township, Hocking County, Ohio. He married GOLDIE ETHEL DONLEY. She was born on 11 Jun 1892 in Laurel Township, Hocking County, Ohio. She died on 19 Mar 1958 in Hocking County, Ohio.

        More About Darl Stahr:
        Burial: 18 Dec 1947 in Mount Olive Cemetery, South Perry, Ohio

Occupation: 1917 in Rockbridge, Hocking County, Ohio; Farmer
Occupation: 1920 in Falls Township, Hocking County, Ohio; Saw Mill
Occupation: 1930 in Laurel Township, Hocking County, Ohio; Odd Jobs
Laborer
Occupation: 1940 in Laurel Township, Hocking County, Ohio; Farmer
Occupation: Lumber Dealer

3   MARTHA THERESA STAHR was born on 22 Jul 1898 in Laurel Township, Hocking County, Ohio. She died on 28 Dec 1903 in Ohio.

More About Martha Theresa Stahr:
Burial: Mount Olive Cemetery, South Perry, Ohio

Notes:

Descendants of James Hutson

Generation 1

1. **JAMES[1] HUTSON** was born about 1802 in Pennsylvania. He died on 17 Mar 1889 in Fox Township, Carroll County, Ohio. He married **ELLENOR CLARK**. She was born about 1805 in Pennsylvania. She died between 28 Sep 1850-25 Nov 1852 in Ohio. He married (2) **MARGARET WALLACE** on 25 Nov 1852 in Carroll County, Ohio. She was born in Feb 1820 in Pennsylvania. She died after 15 Jun 1900.

More About James Hutson:
Living In: Bet. 1840-1880 Fox Township, Carroll County, Ohio
Occupation: Farmer; Fox Township, Carroll County, Ohio

Notes for Ellenor Clark:
Death certificate of John C. Hutson gives her name as Ellen May.

James Hutson and Ellenor Clark had the following children:

    i.   ELIZABETH[2] HUTSON was born about 1832 in Ohio.

    ii. JOHN C. HUTSON was born on 26 Mar 1834 in Carroll County, Ohio. He died on 06 Aug 1921 in Fairfield Township, Columbiana County, Ohio. He married Martha Cross about 1858. She was born in 1838 in Ohio. She died in 1907 in Ohio.

More About John C. Hutson:
Burial: 09 Aug 1921 in Fairfield Cemetery, Fairfield Township, Columbiana County, Ohio
Cause Of Death: Uremia
Living In: 1900 Fairfield Township, Columbiana County, Ohio
Occupation: Farmer

Notes for John C. Hutson:
Death certificate gives March 26, 1834 as birth date. 1900 U.S. census gives February 1833 as birth date. Head Stone gives birth year as 1834.

    iii. PHEBE HUTSON was born on 18 May 1834 in Carroll County, Ohio. She died on 18 Nov 1905 in Lancaster, Ohio. She married Wesley Summers Tucker, son of Henry William Tucker and Anna Roby on 01 May 1856 in Hocking County, Ohio. He was born on 03 Apr 1834 in Leesburg, Carroll County, Ohio. He died on 14 Aug 1906 in Goodhope Township, Hocking County, Ohio.

    SARAH HUTSON was born about 1835 in Ohio.

    SUSANNAH HUTSON was born on 26 Jun 1836 in Ohio. She died on 03 Jan 1904 in Jefferson County, Ohio. She married John Parsons on 03 Jul 1855 in Carroll County, Ohio. He was born in Jul 1834 in Hammondsville, Jefferson County, Ohio. He died on 20 Mar 1905 in Salem Township, Jefferson County, Ohio.

    ELLEN HUTSON was born about 1840 in Ohio.

    LYDIA HUTSON was born about 1842 in Ohio.

    CATHERINE HUTSON was born about 1844 in Ohio.

ix.   RACHAEL HUTSON was born about 1845 in Ohio.

x.   JAMES S. HUTSON was born in 1846 in Ohio. He died in 1930 in Kansas. He married Rebecca Nestrick on 16 Nov 1871 in Carroll County, Ohio. She was born in 1844 in Ohio. She died in 1925 in Kansas.

More About James S. Hutson:
Burial: High Prairie Cemetery, Altoona, Wilson County, Kansas
Military Service: Civil War; 26th Independent Battery, Ohio Light Artillery

More About Margaret Wallace:
Living In: 1900 in With her daughter, Samantha, and her family in East Liverpool, Columbiana County, Ohio

James Hutson and Margaret Wallace had the following children:

xi.   GEORGE W. HUTSON was born in Feb 1855 in Carroll County, Ohio. He died on 25 Oct 1939 in Fox Township, Carroll County, Ohio. He married Sarah Jane Taylor, daughter of William Taylor and Nancy Babbs on 20 Sep 1877 in Carroll County, Ohio. She was born on 12 Feb 1853 in Carroll County, Ohio. She died on 09 Nov 1938 in Monroe Township, Carroll County, Ohio.

More About George W. Hutson:
Burial: 28 Oct 1939 in Mechanicstown Cemetery, Mechanicstown, Carroll County, Ohio
Cause Of Death: Uremic Coma
Occupation: Farmer

Notes for George W. Hutson:
Death certificate gives February 1855 as birth date. 1900 U.S. census gives March 1857 as birth date.

xii.   MARGARET B. HUTSON was born in Oct 1859 in Ohio. She died in 1924 in California. She married John K. House on 23 Sep 1880 in Carroll County, Ohio. He was born on 21 Sep 1859 in Ohio. He died on 24 Jan 1942 in Los Angeles County, California.

More About Margaret B. Hutson:
Burial: Angelus Rosedale Cemetery, Los Angeles, Los Angeles County, California

3.   xiii. SAMANTHA HANNAH HUTSON was born on 22 Feb 1861 in Mechanicstown, Carroll County, Ohio. She died on 26 Oct 1936 in Smith Township, Mahoning County, Ohio. She married Samuel James Baxter, son of James Baxter and Margaret (unknown) on 26 Sep 1885 in Carroll County, Ohio. He was born on 28 Mar 1862 in Carroll County, Ohio. He died on 08 Jul 1948 in Washington Township, Stark County, Ohio.

Generation 2

2.   **PHEBE^2 HUTSON** (James^1) was born on 18 May 1834 in Carroll County, Ohio. She died on 18 Nov 1905 in Lancaster, Ohio. She married Wesley Summers Tucker, son of Henry William Tucker and Anna Roby on 01 May 1856 in Hocking County, Ohio. He was born on 03 Apr 1834 in Leesburg, Carroll County, Ohio. He died on 14 Aug 1906 in Goodhope Township, Hocking County, Ohio.

More About Phebe Hutson:
Burial: Fairview Methodist Church Cemetery, Good Hope Township, Hocking County, Ohio

Notes for Phebe Hutson:
Ohio death index gives birth year as 1834. 1900 U.S. census gives birth date as May 1834. Headstone gives birth year as 1834.

First name is from her headstone.

More About Wesley Summers Tucker:
Burial: Fairview Methodist Church Cemetery, Good Hope Township, Hocking County, Ohio
Living In: 1850 With his half sister, Etheldra, and her family in Dover Township, Tuscarawas County, Ohio.
Living In: 1890 Goodhope Township, Hocking County, Ohio
Occupation: 1850 in Dover Township, Tuscarawas County, Ohio; Chair Maker
Occupation: 1860 in New Lexington, Perry County, Ohio; Carpenter
Occupation: 1870 in Laurel Township, Hocking County, Ohio; Cabinet Maker
Occupation: 1880 in Laurel Township, Hocking County, Ohio; Working on Saw Mill
Occupation: 1900 in Rockbridge, Good Hope Township, Hocking County, Ohio; Proprietor of Planning Mill
Military Service: Bet. 04 Aug 1861-16 Aug 1863 ; Company B, 31st Ohio Infantry, U.S. Army
Property: 1870 in Laurel Township, Hocking County, Ohio; 25 acres Improved and 18 Acres Unimproved

Notes for Wesley Summers Tucker:
Mustered out of the U.S. Army at Camp Thomas, near Columbus, Ohio.

Registered for draft June 1863 in Laurel Township, Hocking County, Ohio.

Wesley Summers Tucker and Phebe Hutson had the following children:

    i. JOSEPH B.[3] TUCKER was born on 02 Feb 1857 in Hocking County, Ohio. He died on 13 Jun 1926 in Columbus, Franklin County, Ohio. He married Nellie May Blackburn, daughter of William Blackburn and Hannah McGraco on 23 Dec 1880 in Hocking County, Ohio. She was born on 15 Aug 1858 in Pickaway County, Ohio. She died on 06 Nov 1935 in Columbus, Franklin County, Ohio.

    More About Joseph B. Tucker:
    Burial: 15 Jun 1926 in Greenlawn Cemetery, Columbus, Franklin County, Ohio
    Living In: 1880 With his parents in Laurel Township, Hocking County, Ohio.
    Occupation: 1870 in Laurel Township, Hocking County, Ohio; Farm Worker
    Occupation: 1880 in Laurel Township, Hocking County, Ohio; Farmer
    Occupation: 1900 in Lancaster, Fairfield County, Ohio; Common Labor
    Occupation: 1910 in Lancaster, Fairfield County, Ohio; General Work Laborer
    Occupation: 1920 in Columbus, Franklin County, Ohio; Railroad Shop Labor

2   HOLLIS CLARK TUCKER was born on 15 Aug 1858 in Hocking County, Ohio. He died on 25 Apr 1916 in Columbus, Franklin County, Ohio. He married (1) CLARA FOX, daughter of Peter Fox and Deborah White on 16 Feb 1879 in Hocking County, Ohio. She was born on 27 Sep 1857 in Laurel Township, Hocking County, Ohio. She died on 30 Dec 1923 in Laurelville, Hocking County, Ohio. He married (2) ELIZA LUCRETIA HULS, daughter of David William Huls and Eliza Ann Peters on 12 Jul 1893 in Hocking County, Ohio. She was born on 19 Jan 1875 in Hocking County,

Ohio. She died on 21 Nov 1960 in Hocking County, Ohio.

More About Hollis Clark Tucker:
Burial: 28 Apr 1916 in Fairview Methodist Church Cemetery, Good Hope
Township, Hocking County, Ohio
Cause Of Death: Punctured lung from fractured ribs due to being run down by a
railroad train.
Occupation: 1870; Farm Worker, Laurel, Ohio
Occupation: 1900 in Rockbridge, Goodhope Township, Hocking County,
Ohio; Derrick Builder
Occupation: 1910 in Goodhope Township, Hocking County, Ohio;
Laborer
Occupation: Carpenter

Notes for Hollis Clark Tucker:
Death certificate gives birth date as August 15, 1854. Age given on death
certificate would give a birth date of August 15, 1858. 1900 U.S. census gives
birthdate as August 1858. Hollis Tucker and Clara Fox marriage license
indicates an 1858 birth.

 iii. SARAH SARVILLA TUCKER was born on 20 May 1860 in New Lexington, Perry County,
Ohio. She died on 04 Jun 1871 in Laurel Township, Hocking County, Ohio.

 iv. BETTY EMMA TUCKER was born on 17 Feb 1862 in Ohio. She died on 01 Oct 1863
in Ohio.

 v. ELLA SOMORRAH TUCKER was born on 09 Mar 1866 in Ohio. She died on 21 Aug
1885 in Tennessee.

  More About Ella Somorrah Tucker:
  Burial: Mount Ararat Cemetery, Lawrence County, Tennessee

 vi. JAMES HENRY TUCKER was born on 25 Apr 1873 in Laurel Township, Hocking County,
Ohio. He died on 27 Feb 1878 in Laurel Township, Hocking County, Ohio.

3. **SAMANTHA HANNAH**[2] **HUTSON** (James[1]) was born on 22 Feb 1861 in Mechanicstown, Carroll
County, Ohio. She died on 26 Oct 1936 in Smith Township, Mahoning County, Ohio. She
married Samuel James Baxter, son of James Baxter and Margaret (unknown) on 26 Sep 1885
in Carroll County, Ohio. He was born on 28 Mar 1862 in Carroll County, Ohio. He died on 08 Jul
1948 in Washington Township, Stark County, Ohio.

More About Samantha Hannah Hutson:
Burial: 28 Oct 1936 in Salem, Columbiana County, Ohio
Cause Of Death: Fractured skull and left hip with shock and hemmorhage after being hit by a
train at a railroad crossing on October 17, 1936.

More About Samuel James Baxter:
Burial: 10 Jul 1948 in Alliance City Cemetery, Alliance, Stark County,
Ohio
Living In: 1900 East Liverpool, Columbiana County, Ohio

Notes for Samuel James Baxter:
Buried beside his second wife.

Samuel James Baxter and Samantha Hannah Hutson had the following children:

    i.   CECIL[3] BAXTER was born in 1888 in Ohio.

    ii.   MAGGIE BAXTER was born in 1892 in Ohio.

    iii.   MYRTLE BAXTER was born in 1895 in Ohio.

Notes:

Descendants of Abraham Delong

Generation 1

1. **ABRAHAM**[1] **DELONG** was born on 01 Jan 1773 in Pennsylvania. He died on 03 Nov 1859 in Allen County, Ohio. He married Johannah Steman, daughter of Christian Steman and Hannah Barr in Fayette County, Pennsylvania. She was born on 10 May 1788 in Rockingham County, Virginia. She died in 1875 in Allen County, Ohio.

More About Abraham Delong:
Occupation: 1850 in Marion Township, Hocking County, Ohio; Farmer

More About Johannah Steman:
Living In: 1860 With her son, Isaac, and his family in Logan Township, Auglaize County, Ohio.
Living In: 1870 With her son, Isaac, and his family in German Township, Allen County, Ohio.

Abraham Delong and Johannah Steman had the following children:

   i. SAMUEL FRANKLIN[2] DELONG was born about 1803 in Pennsylvania. He died after 20 Aug 1870 in Hocking County, Ohio. He married (1) MARY ANN KIMBLE on 14 Aug 1825 in Laurel Township, Hocking County, Ohio. She was born in 1805 in Fairfield County, Ohio. She died on 15 Nov 1862 in Hocking County, Ohio. He married (2) ELIZABETH STERNS, daughter of John Sterns and Mary (unknown) on 02 Mar 1865 in Hocking County, Ohio. She was born about 1816 in Pennsylvania. She died on 22 Dec 1891 in Columbus, Franklin County, Ohio.

   MARGARET DELONG was born about 1809 in Pennsylvania.

   More About Margaret Delong:
   Living In: 1850 With her parents in Marion Township, Hocking County, Ohio.
   Living In: 1860 With her brother, Isaac, and his family in Logan Township, Auglaize County, Ohio.
   Living In: 1870 With her brother, Isaac, and his family in German Township, Allen County, Ohio.

   JOHN DELONG was born about 1811 in Pennsylvania. He married Mary Magdalene Spohn on 03 Jun 1834 in Fairfield County, Ohio. She was born about 1812 in Ohio.

   More About John Delong:
   Occupation: 1850 in Marion Township, Hocking County, Ohio; Farmer

   CHRISTIAN DELONG was born about 1813 in Ohio. He married Hannah Beery on 20 Mar 1845 in Fairfield County, Ohio. She was born about 1810 in Virginia.

   More About Christian Delong:
   Occupation: 1850 in Marion Township, Hocking County, Ohio; Farmer

   v. CATHERINE DELONG was born on 20 Apr 1816 in Ohio. She died on 30 Oct 1893 in Duchouquet Township, Auglaize County, Ohio. She married Samuel Moyer on 17 Jan 1837 in Allen County, Ohio. He was born on 10 Jul 1813 in Ohio. He died on 22 Jan 1905 in Duchouquet Township, Auglaize County, Ohio.

   DANIEL DELONG was born about 1818 in Ohio. He died after 08 Jun 1880. He married (1) NANCY REED on 11 Aug 1839 in Fairfield County, Ohio. She was born about 1820 in Ohio. He married (2) HANNAH CAFFITZ on 22 Aug 1869 in Fairfield

County, Ohio. She was born about 1822 in Pennsylvania.

More About Daniel Delong:
Occupation: 1850 in Hocking Township, Fairfield County, Ohio; Plasterer

vii.   ABRAHAM DELONG was born about 1821 in Ohio. He married (1) ELIZABETH MOWRY on 26 Nov 1843 in Hocking County, Ohio. She was born about 1827 in Ohio. He married (2) CATHERINE MOWRY on 25 May 1854 in Hocking County, Ohio. She was born about 1825 in Ohio.

More About Abraham Delong:
Occupation: 1850 in Marion Township, Hocking County, Ohio; Farmer

viii.   ANNA MAGDALENA DELONG was born in Apr 1823 in Ohio. She died on 25 Feb 1907 in Spencerville, Allen County, Ohio. She married Cornelius Stoneburner on 02 Mar 1843 in Fairfield County, Ohio. He was born about 1821 in Ohio. He died on 11 Feb 1895 in Spencer Township, Allen county, Ohio.

ix.   HANNAH DELONG was born on 29 Jun 1825 in Ohio. She died on 13 May 1886 in Logan Township, Auglaize County, Ohio. She married JOSEPH PIERSON. He was born on 18 Nov 1826 in Fairfield County, Ohio. He died on 04 Mar 1900 in Logan Township, Auglaize County, Ohio.

More About Hannah Delong:
Burial: Allentown Cemetery, Allentown, Allen county, Ohio

Notes for Hannah Delong:
Birth date is from age at death on death record.
----

x.   ISAAC DELONG was born about 1828 in Ohio. He died on 26 Apr 1899 in Crotty, Coffey County, Kansas. He married (1) MARY ANN SPOHN on 26 Oct 1851 in Franklin County, Ohio. She was born about 1829 in Ohio. He married (2) MINERVA A. REED on 04 Jul 1888 in Coffey County, Kansas. She was born about 1849.

More About Isaac Delong:
Burial: Big Creek Cemetery, Burlington, Coffey County, Kansas
Living In: 1850 Living with his parents in Marion Township, Hocking County, Ohio.
Occupation: 1860 in Logan Township, Auglaize County, Ohio; Farmer
Occupation: 1870 in German Township, Allen County, Ohio; Farmer

xi.   LYDIA DELONG was born about 1841 in Ohio.

Generation 2

2   SAMUEL FRANKLIN[2] DELONG (Abraham[1]) was born about 1803 in Pennsylvania. He died after 20 Aug 1870 in Hocking County, Ohio. He married (1) MARY ANN KIMBLE on 14 Aug 1825 in Laurel Township, Hocking County, Ohio. She was born in 1805 in Fairfield County, Ohio. She died on 15 Nov 1862 in Hocking County, Ohio. He married (2) ELIZABETH STERNS, daughter of John Sterns and Mary (unknown) on 02 Mar 1865 in Hocking County, Ohio. She was born about 1816 in

Pennsylvania. She died on 22 Dec 1891 in Columbus, Franklin County, Ohio.

More About Samuel Franklin Delong:
Occupation: 1850 in Laurel Township, Hocking County, Ohio; Farmer
Occupation: 1860 in Laurel Township, Hocking County, Ohio; Farmer
Occupation: 1870 in Perry Township, Hocking County, Ohio; Post Master

Samuel Franklin Delong and Mary Ann Kimble had the following children:

4.   i. SOLOMON[3] DELONG was born about 1826 in Laurel Township, Hocking County, Ohio. He married Mary Ellen Brown on 17 Oct 1844 in Fairfield County, Ohio. She was born about 1824 in Virginia. She died after 20 Jun 1900.

5.   ii. JOHN DELONG was born on 03 Apr 1829 in Laurel Township, Hocking County, Ohio. He died on 21 Feb 1884 in Givens, Pike County, Ohio. He married (1) MARY FOX on 24 Nov 1850 in Hocking County, Ohio. She was born on 26 Apr 1835 in Ohio. She died on 05 Nov 1852. He married (2) DELILAH VAN CUREN on 03 Jul 1853 in Hocking County, Ohio. She was born in Sep 1833 in Ohio. She died after 08 Jun 1900.

6.   iii. MARY ELIZABETH DELONG was born on 19 Jan 1831 in Laurel Township, Hocking County, Ohio. She died on 30 Jun 1877 in Hocking County, Ohio. She married Isaac Bigham, son of Samuel Bigham and Sarah Morris on 16 Apr 1850 in Hocking County, Ohio. He was born on 10 Mar 1828 in Guernsey County, Ohio. He died on 29 Nov 1896 in Laurel Township, Hocking County, Ohio.

7   iv. SAMUEL JACKSON DELONG was born in 1833 in Laurel Township, Hocking County, Ohio. He died on 25 May 1864 in Georgia. He married Nancy McCaslin on 06 Mar 1856 in Hocking County, Ohio. She was born in Ohio.

8   v. JOSIAH DELONG was born on 04 Jan 1835 in Laurel Township, Hocking County, Ohio. He died on 24 Sep 1916 in Perkins Township, Erie County, Ohio. He married (1) MARY ELIZABETH JULIEN, daughter of Alexander Julien and Elenor Clendenin on 5 Nov 1857 in Hocking County, Ohio. She was born on 13 Mar 1840 in Ohio. She died on 19 Mar 1880 in Ohio. He married (2) MARY CAROLINE WALTNER on 07 Oct 1880 in Putnam County, Ohio. He married (3) MARY J. WELLS on 30 Nov 1884 in Fairfield County, Ohio. She was born in 1858. She died in 1897. He married (4) FRANCES CLARA SHANK, daughter of John Shank and Fannie Everette on 29 Mar 1900 in Hocking County, Ohio. She was born on 19 Jan 1846 in South Perry, Hocking County, Ohio. She died on 17 Sep 1936 in Perry Township, Hocking County, Ohio.

9   vi. EVELINE DELONG was born on 02 Nov 1836 in Laurel Township, Hocking County, Ohio. She died on 09 Jul 1909 in Lancaster, Fairfield County, Ohio. She married Sampson Friend, son of George Friend and Sarah (unknown) on 30 Dec 1854 in Hocking County, Ohio. He was born on 23 Apr 1834 in Ohio. He died in 1896 in Ohio.

10   vii. JOSEPH DELONG was born on 23 Apr 1839 in Laurel Township, Hocking County, Ohio. He died on 09 Dec 1891 in Goodhope Township, Hocking County, Ohio. He married Catherine Woltz, daughter of Thomas Woltz and Nancy Sutton on 01 Dec 1859 in Hocking County, Ohio. She was born on 03 Jul 1839 in Hocking County, Ohio. She died on 12 Dec 1929 in Lancaster, Fairfield County, Ohio.

11   viii. CALISTA ANN DELONG was born on 01 Nov 1841 in Laurel Township, Hocking County, Ohio. She died on 07 Aug 1901 in Ohio. She married JOHN F. THOMPSON. She married (2) MAURICE KANE on 17 Jun 1860 in Hocking County, Ohio. He was

born on 23 Jul 1819 in Fairfield County, Ohio. He died on 02 Dec 1879 in Perry Township, Hocking County, Ohio. She married (3) JOHN ROTH between 15 Jun 1880-16 Mar 1884. He died before 23 Jun 1900.

12.   ix. MALINDA DELONG was born on 26 Mar 1844 in Laurel Township, Hocking County, Ohio. She died on 12 Jun 1920 in Wyandotte, Wayne County, Michigan. She married Louis L. Smyers, son of John Smyers on 03 Mar 1864 in Hocking County, Ohio. He was born on 23 Feb 1832 in Ohio. He died on 09 Sep 1915 in Wyandotte, Wayne County, Michigan.

13.   x. JAMES DELONG was born on 06 Jan 1847 in Laurel Township, Hocking County, Ohio. He died on 04 Mar 1912 in Pleasant Township, Fairfield County, Ohio. He married (1) ADIAN ANN CAVE, daughter of Michael Cave and Sarah Moore on 05 Jan 1867 in Hocking County, Ohio. She was born in Jun 1847 in Ohio. She died on 25 Dec 1933 in Derby, Darby Township, Pickaway County, Ohio. He married (2) MARGARETTA KANE, daughter of Maurice Kane and Elizabeth McDowell on 08 Mar 1874 in Fairfield County, Ohio. She was born on 07 Feb 1852 in Hocking County, Ohio. She died on 09 Jul 1938 in Lancaster, Fairfield County, Ohio.

14.   xi. MINERVA JANE DELONG was born on 19 Mar 1852 in Laurel Township, Hocking County, Ohio. She died on 02 Oct 1915 in Lancaster, Fairfield County, Ohio. She married (1) JAMES RAYMOND on 29 Nov 1868 in Hocking County, Ohio. He was born about 1847 in Ohio. She married (2) ELIAS POTTS on 23 Oct 1877 in Fairfield County, Ohio.

More About Elizabeth Sterns:
Burial: 24 Dec 1891 in Green Lawn Cemetery, Columbus, Franklin County, Ohio
Occupation: 1860 in Logan, Hocking County, Ohio; Tavern Keeper

4.   CATHERINE^2 DELONG (Abraham^1) was born on 20 Apr 1816 in Ohio. She died on 30 Oct 1893 in Duchouquet Township, Auglaize County, Ohio. She married Samuel Moyer on 17 Jan 1837 in Allen County, Ohio. He was born on 10 Jul 1813 in Ohio. He died on 22 Jan 1905 in Duchouquet Township, Auglaize County, Ohio.

More About Catherine Delong:
Burial: Saint Matthew Cemetery, Lima, Allen County, Ohio

More About Samuel Moyer:
Burial: Saint Matthew Cemetery, Lima, Allen County, Ohio

Samuel Moyer and Catherine Delong had the following children:

i   ISRAEL^3 MOYER was born on 02 Mar 1845 in Duchouquet Township, Auglaize County, Ohio. He died on 08 Mar 1921 in Duchouquet Township, Auglaize County, Ohio. He married ELIZABETH (UNKNOWN). She was born in 1838. She died in 1926.

More About Israel Moyer:
Burial: 10 Mar 1921 in Saint Matthew Cemetery, Lima, Allen County, Ohio

ii   JOHN F. MOYER was born on 20 Jul 1853 in Cridersville, Auglaize County, Ohio. He died on 04 Dec 1923 in Columbus, Franklin County, Ohio. He married ALICE WILLIAMS.

More About John F. Moyer:

Burial: 06 Dec 1923 in Cridersville, Auglaize County, Ohio

Generation 3

iv.   **SOLOMON**[3] **DELONG** (Samuel Franklin[2], Abraham[1]) was born about 1826 in Laurel Township, Hocking County, Ohio. He married Mary Ellen Brown on 17 Oct 1844 in Fairfield County, Ohio. She was born about 1824 in Virginia. She died after 20 Jun 1900.

More About Solomon Delong:
Occupation: 1850 in Perry Township, Hocking County, Ohio; Farmer
Occupation: 1860 in Perry Township, Hocking County, Ohio; Farmer
Occupation: 1870 in Laurel Township, Hocking County, Ohio; Day Laborer

More About Mary Ellen Brown:
Living In: 1900 With her daughter, Louisa, and her family in Ridge Township, Shelby County, Illinois.

Solomon Delong and Mary Ellen Brown had the following children:

ELIZABETH[4] DELONG was born about 1845 in Ohio.

WILLIAM DELONG was born about 1847 in Ohio.

LOUISA DELONG was born on 17 Jun 1852 in Ohio. She died on 20 Feb 1933 in Nokomis, Montgomery County, Illinois.

More About Louisa Delong:
Burial: 23 Feb 1933 in Oak Grove Cemetery, Nokomis, Montgomery County, Illinois

Notes for Louisa Delong:
Married 1st - Newton Kirkbride, 2nd - LeRoy Stanley, 3rd - William Miller, 4th Oscar Landon.

CATHERINE DELONG was born about 1855 in Ohio.

CRISTA DELONG was born about 1859 in Ohio.

MATILDA M. DELONG was born about 1864 in Ohio.

GEORGE DELONG was born about 1867 in Ohio.

v.   **JOHN**[3] **DELONG** (Samuel Franklin[2], Abraham[1]) was born on 03 Apr 1829 in Laurel Township, Hocking County, Ohio. He died on 21 Feb 1884 in Givens, Pike County, Ohio. He married (1) **MARY FOX** on 24 Nov 1850 in Hocking County, Ohio. She was born on 26 Apr 1835 in Ohio. She died on 05 Nov 1852. He married (2) **DELILAH VAN CUREN** on 03 Jul 1853 in Hocking County, Ohio. She was born in Sep 1833 in Ohio. She died after 08 Jun 1900.

More About John Delong:
Burial: Givens Chapel Cemetery, Givens, Pike County, Ohio
Occupation: 1860 in Madison Township, Fairfield County, Ohio; Farmer
Occupation: 1870 in Madison Township, Fairfield County, Ohio; Farm Laborer
Occupation: 1880 in Circleville Township, Pickaway County, Ohio; Laborer

Military Service: Civil War; Company D, 58th Ohio Infantry

More About Mary Fox:
Burial: Brown Cemetery, Goodhope Township, Hocking County, Ohio

John Delong and Mary Fox had the following child:

    i.   HARRIET[4] DELONG was born on 25 Apr 1851 in Hocking County, Ohio. She died on 02 Nov 1940 in Flushing Township, Belmont County, Ohio. She married WILLIAM C. THOMPSON. He was born on 03 Nov 1850 in Ohio. He died on 04 Apr 1921 in Flushing Township, Belmont County, Ohio.

        More About Harriet Delong:
        Burial: 04 Nov 1940 in Union Cemetery, Flushing, Belmont County, Ohio

More About Delilah Van Curen:
Living In: 1900 With her daughter, Elizabeth, and her family in Johnson Township, Champaign County, Ohio.

John Delong and Delilah Van Curen had the following children:

    ii.   JACOB DELONG was born about 1854 in Ohio.

    iii.   CATHERINE DELONG was born about 1856 in Ohio.

    iv.   JOHN DELONG was born about 1858 in Ohio.

    v.   WILLIAM DELONG was born about Dec 1859 in Ohio.

    vi.   ALLEN DELONG was born on 29 May 1864 in Ohio. He died on 15 Sep 1941 in Madison Township, Clark County, Ohio. He married ANNA (UNKNOWN).

        More About Allen Delong:
        Burial: 18 Sep 1941 in Mechanicsburg, Ohio

    vii.   ANDREW DELONG was born about 1867 in Ohio.

    viii.   CHARLES DELONG was born about 1869 in Ohio.

    ix.   JANE DELONG was born about 1872 in Ohio.

    x.   ELIZABETH DELONG was born in Jun 1876 in Ohio. She married JAMES F. GILES. He was born in May 1868 in Pennsylvania.

6   **MARY ELIZABETH[3] DELONG** (Samuel Franklin[2], Abraham[1]) was born on 19 Jan 1831 in Laurel Township, Hocking County, Ohio. She died on 30 Jun 1877 in Hocking County, Ohio. She married Isaac Bigham, son of Samuel Bigham and Sarah Morris on 16 Apr 1850 in Hocking County, Ohio. He was born on 10 Mar 1828 in Guernsey County, Ohio. He died on 29 Nov 1896 in Laurel Township, Hocking County, Ohio.

More About Mary Elizabeth Delong:
Burial: Betheny Church Cemetery, Hocking County, Ohio

More About Isaac Bigham:
Burial: Brown Cemetery, Good Hope Township, Hocking County, Ohio
Occupation: 1850 in Good Hope Township, Hocking County, Ohio; Farmer
Occupation: 1860 in Laurel Township, Hocking County, Ohio; Farmer
Occupation: 1870 in Laurel Township, Hocking County, Ohio; Farmer
Occupation: 1880 in Laurel Township, Hocking County, Ohio; Farmer

Isaac Bigham and Mary Elizabeth Delong had the following children:

1. ABRAHAM[4] BIGHAM was born on 03 Jul 1849 in Hocking County, Ohio. He died on
    02 May 1931 in Perry Township, Hocking County, Ohio. He married (1) MARGARET
    BYERS, daughter of John S. Byers and Nancy Eaton on 13 Oct 1870 in Hocking
    County, Ohio. He married (2) SEENITH CROY on 22 Sep 1877 in Hocking County,
    Ohio. She was born in May 1853 in Ohio. He married (3) MATILDA MCGRADY,
    daughter of Unknown and Ellen McGrady on 15 Apr 1914. She was born on 29
    Jan 1869 in Hocking County, Ohio. She died on 25 Nov 1941 in Perry Township,
    Hocking County, Ohio.

    More About Abraham Bigham:
    Burial: 04 May 1931 in Pisgah Church Cemetery, Hocking County,
    Ohio Cause Of Death: Cardiac Insufficiency
    Occupation: Farmer

2. SAMUEL BIGHAM was born on 11 Oct 1851 in Hocking County, Ohio. He died on 16
    Jan 1922 in Lancaster, Fairfield County, Ohio. He married Charlotte E. Teeter,
    daughter of Curtis W. Teeter and Mary Essford on 16 Sep 1871 in Hocking
    County, Ohio. She was born on 27 Oct 1848 in Newark, Licking County, Ohio.
    She died on 24 Apr 1910 in Lancaster, Fairfield County, Ohio.

    More About Samuel Bigham:
    Burial: 19 Jan 1922 in Brown Cemetery, Goodhope Township, Hocking County,
    Ohio
    Cause Of Death: Chronic Myocarditis
    Occupation: Farmer

iii. WILLIAM BIGHAM was born on 09 Jan 1852 in Hocking County, Ohio. He died on
    15 Jun 1918 in Pleasant Township, Fairfield County, Ohio. He married Rebecca
    Ann Croy, daughter of Samuel Croy and Eliza Bobo on 25 Oct 1875 in Hocking
    County, Ohio. She was born on 06 Apr 1854 in Athens, Ohio. She died on 06
    May 1945 in Logan, Ohio.

    More About William Bigham:
    Burial: 17 Jun 1918 in Betheny Church Cemetery, Hocking County,
    Ohio Cause Of Death: Aortic Stenosis
    Occupation: Farmer

iv. MARY ANN BIGHAM was born on 15 Feb 1855 in Hocking County, Ohio. She died
    on 07 Aug 1924 in Greenfield Township, Fairfield County, Ohio. She married (1)
    LEVI DAVIS, son of Levi Davis and Mary Ann Rodman on 10 Mar 1875 in Hocking
    County, Ohio. He was born on 11 May 1839 in Muskingum County, ohio. He died
    on 08 Apr 1909 in Perry Township, Hocking County, Ohio. She married (2)
    NATHANIEL P. SPRINGER, son of John Springer between 08 Apr 1909-04 May 1910.
    He was born on 24 May 1827 in Perry County, Ohio. He died on 28 Oct 1922 in
    Perry Township, Hocking County, Ohio. She married (3) WILLIAM WALTON, son of
    Boaz Walton and Margaret Burress on 27 Sep 1923 in Franklin County, Ohio. He

was born on 17 Aug 1844 in New Philadelphia, Tuscarawas County, Ohio. He died on 19 Feb 1930 in Benton Township, Hocking County, Ohio.

More About Mary Ann Bigham:
Burial: 10 Aug 1924 in Pisgah Church Cemetery, Hocking County,
Ohio Cause Of Death: Addisons Disease
Living In: 1924 Lancaster, Fairfield County, Ohio

v.   SARAH BIGHAM was born on 18 Oct 1856 in Hocking County, Ohio. She died on 30 Apr 1926 in Washington Township, Hocking County, Ohio. She married (1) DANIEL NIXON on 27 Oct 1887 in Hocking County, Ohio. He was born on 13 Nov 1825 in Ohio. He died on 09 Nov 1907 in Athens County, Ohio. She married (2) JAMES FOX, son of James Fox and Nancy Clutter on 23 Jan 1873 in Hocking County, Ohio. He was born on 11 Oct 1851 in Hocking County, Ohio. He died on 14 Jul 1884 in Laurel Township, Hocking County, Ohio.

More About Sarah Bigham:
Burial: 03 May 1926 in Ewing Cemetery, Ewing, Hocking County, Ohio

vi.   ELIZA BIGHAM was born about 1858 in Hocking County, Ohio. She died after 01 Jun 1870.

Notes   for   Eliza
Bigham: Died young.

vii. BYRON BIGHAM was born about Mar 1860 in Hocking County, Ohio. He died before 01 Jun 1870.

viii. ISAAC WESLEY BIGHAM was born on 26 Apr 1861 in Hocking County, Ohio. He died on 01 Feb 1923 in Perry Township, Hocking County, Ohio. He married Zelda Clapper, daughter of Jacob Clapper and Savilla Bowman on 11 Aug 1881 in Hocking County, Ohio. She was born on 05 Feb 1858 in Hocking County, Ohio. She died on 03 Nov 1922 in Perry Township, Hocking County, Ohio.

More About Isaac Wesley Bigham:
Burial: 04 Feb 1923 in Pisgah Church Cemetery, Hocking County,
Ohio Cause Of Death: Organic Heart Trouble
Occupation: Farmer

ix.   JACOB BIGHAM was born on 03 Nov 1862 in Hocking County, Ohio. He died on 20 Aug 1928 in Laurel, Hocking County, Ohio. He married Rachel Deborah Seesholtz, daughter of Henry G. Seesholtz and Catherine Ebert on 14 Feb 1883 in Hocking County, Ohio. She was born on 11 Nov 1863 in South Perry, Hocking County, Ohio. She died on 24 Oct 1951 in Sugar Grove, Fairfield County, Ohio.

More About Jacob Bigham:
Burial: 22 Aug 1928 in Forest Rose Cemetery, Lancaster, Fairfield County,
Ohio Cause Of Death: Septocemia
Occupation: Farmer

x.   JOSEPH BIGHAM was born on 11 May 1863 in Hocking County, Ohio. He died on 24

Jul 1895 in Perry Township, Hocking County, Ohio. He married Louisa Anna Hendrickson, daughter of George Hendrickson and Mary Leisure on 03 Apr 1886 in Hocking County, Ohio. She was born on 12 Apr 1867 in Hocking County, Ohio. She died on 14 Jan 1899 in Perry Township, Hocking County, Ohio.

More About Joseph Bigham:
Burial: Pisgah Church Cemetery, Good Hope Township, Hocking County, Ohio

Notes for Joseph Bigham: Headstone
has 1896 for year of death.

Bigham and Benway
 by Konrad Stump, contributing writer to The Logan Daily News.

In each of our family histories, there are stories we have heard that stick with us, a lot of the time because they involve something that isn't quite explained or understood. Sometimes they are mentioned in passing, and sometimes the stories are known but there are elements that have been told incorrectly. The descendants of Joseph Bigham and Oliver Benway may know something of the story of their deaths, but we'd all like an account of the stories that have been passed down in pieces.

It was Wednesday, July 24, 1895. It was about 9 a.m. At his home in the northwestern part of Laurel Township, near Cantwell Cliffs, Joseph Bigham had been digging a well. He was preparing to build a new house, having made the excavation for the cellar and starting work on this well. He was being assisted but his brother-in-law, Oliver Benway. The evening before, they fired a blast in the well in order to get fire to burn in it, but it didn't do any good. They left the house about seven o'clock on Wednesday morning to work on the well. Joseph went down in the well, but was overcome by carbonic acid gas, which at the time was commonly called well damp. He called to Oliver to pull him up, but was too affected by the gas to hold the rope. Oliver called out for help. Mary Yantes, who was staying with the Bighams at the time, and Joseph's wife Anna, came to assist. Oliver lowered himself into the well, fanning Joseph for a few minutes in an attempt to revive him, but soon felt himself being overcome by the gas. He called for the women to pull him up; they were able to get him up about 16 to 17 feet, but he was so overcome by the gas he fell back to the bottom of the well, which at the time was about 35 feet deep.

Mary ran to the nearest neighbors about a half-mile away, and a group of men came back with her to assist. Dan Kline went down in the well to retrieve the men, but only got about half way before the gas overcame him and he needed to be pulled out. They pumped air into the well by means of a windmill and sheet, and a burning sheaf of wheat was lowered into it. Dan went back down in the bucket, tied a rope around the bodies of Joseph and Oliver, and brought them up. They had been dead for some time, it having been over an hour since Oliver first called for help. Oliver's head was badly cut from when he'd fallen back into the well.

The funerals took place at Mt. Pisgah, with the Rev. Mather officiating. Mather's sermon was delivered outside, as the people who'd come to attend the funerals couldn't fit in the church. People who were there guessed the attendees numbered around one thousand.

Here is what I can tell you of their lives. Joseph was born on May 11, 1863, in Hocking County to Isaac and Mary (Delong) Bigham. He grew up in Laurel

Township, and his father worked as a farmer. On Apr 3, 1886, he married Louisa Anna Hendrickson, daughter of George and Mary (Leisure) Hendrickson. Together they had four children: Samuel Edison, Metta (who died as an infant), Alvah Medred, and Goldie Theresa. Joseph's wife, Anna, remarried to Samuel Lutz on Oct. 6, 1898, and the children surely lived with them along with Samuel's daughter from a previous marriage. However, on Jan. 14, 1899, Anna passed away. Though we can't be sure of a reason, Joseph and Anna's children were spread out by the 1900 federal census. Samuel went to live with Anna's brother, Frank. Alvah went to live with Salem and Samantha Shoemaker, and worked as a servant. Goldie went to live with two of Anna's sisters, Mary and Lavina.

Oliver Benway was born in Canada on Dec. 20, 1861. By 1880, he was living in Antrim County, Michigan, with his brother William. Their father had passed away, but their mother, Louisa, was living with them. On Oct. 27, 1884, Oliver married Elizabeth Della Bigham in Michigan. According to his obituary, Louisa lost her life in a fire not long after his marriage, and Oliver and Elizabeth moved back to Hocking County. The time of this can gauged by the births of Oliver and Elizabeth's children. They had four daughters together: Lydia, Lauretta, Minnie, and Nettie. Minnie was born in Michigan in 1892, and Nettie was born in Good Hope Township in 1894, making the move probably in 1893 or early 1894. After Oliver's death, Elizabeth remarried to Andrew Roop, on Apr. 22, 1897, in Hocking County. Andrew adopted Elizabeth's four daughters, and he and Elizabeth had four sons of their own. The last of these sons was named Oliver.

----

11   NELSON IGNACIUS BIGHAM was born on 09 Feb 1866 in Hocking County, Ohio. He died on 14 Dec 1936 in Laurel Township, Hocking County, Ohio. He married Eliza Jane Friend, daughter of Lorenzo Corbin Friend and Hannah Elizabeth Odell on 17 Apr 1888 in Hocking County, Ohio. She was born on 11 Sep 1868 in Hocking County, Ohio. She died on 02 May 1933 in Laurel Township, Hocking County, Ohio.

More About Nelson Ignacius Bigham:
Burial: 17 Dec 1936 in Fairview Methodist Church Cemetery, Good Hope Township, Hocking County, Ohio
Cause Of Death: Heart Disease
Occupation: Farmer

12   NANCY MARGARET BIGHAM was born on 09 Feb 1867 in Laurel Township, Hocking County, Ohio. She died on 24 Sep 1870 in Laurel Townshiop, Hocking County, Ohio.

More About Nancy Margaret Bigham:
Burial: Betheny Church Cemetery, Hocking County, Ohio Cause Of Death: Burned to Death

13   ELIZABETH DELLA BIGHAM was born on 11 Mar 1870 in Hocking County, Ohio. She

died on 23 Aug 1952 in Rockbridge, Hocking County, Ohio. She married (1)
OLIVER BENWAY on 27 Oct 1884 in Central Lake, Antrim County, Michigan. He was
born on 27 Dec 1861 in Canada. He died on 24 Jul 1895 in Good Hope
Township, Hocking County, Ohio. She married (2) ANDREW MARTIN ROOP, son of
Martin Roop and Elizabeth Springer on 22 Apr 1897 in Hocking County, Ohio. He
was born on 19 Mar 1869 in Good Hope Township, Hocking County, Ohio. He
died on 22 Nov 1950 in Rockbridge, Hocking County, Ohio.

More About Elizabeth Della Bigham:
Burial: 26 Aug 1952 in Fairview Memorial Gardens, Rockbridge, Hocking County,
Ohio
Cause Of Death: ; Cerebral Hemorrhage

7. SAMUEL JACKSON[3] DELONG (Samuel Franklin[2], Abraham[1]) was born in 1833 in Laurel Township,
Hocking County, Ohio. He died on 25 May 1864 in Georgia. He married Nancy McCaslin on 06
Mar 1856 in Hocking County, Ohio. She was born in Ohio.

More About Samuel Jackson Delong:
Living In: 1863 Madison Township, Fairfield County, Ohio
Occupation: 1860 in Madison Township, Fairfield County, Ohio; Day Laborer Military
Service: Bet. 31 Mar-25 May 1864 ; Company I, 73rd Ohio Infantry, U.S.A.

Notes for Samuel Jackson Delong:
Killed in action May 25, 1864 during the battle of New Hope Church in Georgia.

Samuel Jackson Delong and Nancy McCaslin had the following children:

 i. SUSANNA[4] DELONG was born on 26 Apr 1857 in Ohio. She died on 13 May 1925 in
San Antonio, Bexar County, Texas. She married Allen Pearce on 22 Feb 1876 in Fairfield County,
Ohio. He died before 13 May 1925.

  More About Susanna Delong:
  Burial: Pickerington, Ohio

 ii. PERRY A. DELONG was born about Jul 1860 in Madison Township, Fairfield County,
Ohio.

 iii. SAMUEL B. DELONG was born on 03 Sep 1862 in Madison Township, Fairfield
County, Ohio.

8. JOSIAH[3] DELONG (Samuel Franklin[2], Abraham[1]) was born on 04 Jan 1835 in Laurel Township,
Hocking County, Ohio. He died on 24 Sep 1916 in Perkins Township, Erie County, Ohio. He
married (1) MARY ELIZABETH JULIEN, daughter of Alexander Julien and Elenor Clendenin on 05
Nov 1857 in Hocking County, Ohio. She was born on 13 Mar 1840 in Ohio. She died on 19 Mar
1880 in Ohio. He married (2) MARY CAROLINE WALTNER on 07 Oct 1880 in Putnam County, Ohio.
He married (3) MARY J. WELLS on 30 Nov 1884 in Fairfield County, Ohio. She was born in 1858.
She died in 1897. He married (4) FRANCES CLARA SHANK, daughter of John Shank and Fannie
Everette on 29 Mar 1900 in Hocking County, Ohio. She was born on 19 Jan 1846 in South Perry,
Hocking County, Ohio. She died on 17 Sep 1936 in Perry Township, Hocking County, Ohio.

More About Josiah Delong:

Burial: 25 Sep 1916 in Elmwood Cemetery, Lancaster, Fairfield County,
Ohio Living In: 1890 Columbus Grove, Putnam County, Ohio
Occupation: 1860 in Madison Township, Fairfield County, Ohio; Day Laborer
Occupation: 1870 in Amanda Township, Fairfield County, Ohio; Farm Laborer
Occupation: 1880 in Columbus Grove, Putnam County, Ohio; Day Laborer
Occupation: 1900 in Worthington, Franklin County, Ohio; Farmer
Occupation: 1910 in Greenfield Township, Fairfield County, Ohio; Farm Laborer, Odd Jobs
Military Service: Bet. 28 Feb 1864-10 May 1865 ; Company B, 31st Ohio Infantry, U.S. Army

Notes for Josiah Delong:
Mustered out of Company B, 31st Ohio Infantry on May 10, 1865 at Camp Dennison, Ohio.

Died at State Soldiers Home.

More About Mary Elizabeth Julien:
Burial: Bogart Cemetery, Columbus Grove, Putnam County, Ohio

Josiah Delong and Mary Elizabeth Julien had the following children:

      i. ELLEN ISABELL[4] DELONG was born on 26 Jun 1859 in Hocking County, Ohio. She died
         on 01 Aug 1940 in Columbus, Franklin County, Ohio. She married Isaac
         Neiswander on 08 Nov 1874 in Fairfield County, Ohio.

         More About Ellen Isabell Delong:
         Burial: 03 Aug 1940 in Obetz Cemetery, Obetz, Franklin County, Ohio

     ii.   BURRELL C. DELONG was born on 10 Feb 1862 in Ohio. He died on 03 Apr 1914
         in Columbus, Franklin County, Ohio.

         More About Burrell C. Delong:
         Burial: 05 Apr 1914 in Mifflin Cemetery, Gahanna, Franklin County, Ohio
         Cause Of Death: Tuberculosis

More About Frances Clara Shank:
Burial: 30 Sep 1936 in Betheny Church Cemetery, Perry Township, Hocking County, Ohio
Living In: 1930 With her brother, William Shank, in Perry Township, Hocking County, Ohio.

Notes for Frances Clara Shank:
Name and birthdate are on headstone with Josiah Delong in Elmwood Cemetery, Lancaster,
Ohio but she is buried in Betheny Cemetery, Perry Township, Hocking County, Ohio.
----

9   EVELINE[3] DELONG (Samuel Franklin[2], Abraham[1]) was born on 02 Nov 1836 in Laurel Township,
    Hocking County, Ohio. She died on 09 Jul 1909 in Lancaster, Fairfield County, Ohio. She
    married Sampson Friend, son of George Friend and Sarah (unknown) on 30 Dec 1854 in
    Hocking County, Ohio. He was born on 23 Apr 1834 in Ohio. He died in 1896 in Ohio.

    More About Eveline Delong:
    Burial: Forest Rose Cemetery, Lancaster, Fairfield County, Ohio

    More About Sampson Friend:

Burial: Forest Rose Cemetery, Lancaster, Fairfield County,
Ohio
Living In: 1890 Lancaster, Fairfield County, Ohio
Occupation: 1860 in Perry Township, Hocking County, Ohio; Laborer
Occupation: 1870 in Clear Creek Township, Fairfield County, Ohio; Farm
Laborer
Occupation: 1880 in Hocking Township, Fairfield County, Ohio; Laborer
Military Service: Bet. 24 Jun 1864-19 Jun 1865; Company I, 122nd Ohio Infantry, U.S.A.

Notes for Sampson Friend:
Mustered out of U.S. Army on June 19, 1865 at Washington D.C.

Sampson Friend and Eveline Delong had the following children:

     i.   MARY ANN[4] FRIEND was born about 1855 in Ohio.

     ii.   MINERVA JANE FRIEND was born about 1857 in Ohio.

     iii.   CALISTA E. FRIEND was born about 1859 in Ohio.

     iv.   THOMAS FRIEND was born about 1862 in Ohio.

     v.   HENRIETTA FRIEND was born about 1866 in Ohio.

     vi.   EMMA FRIEND was born about 1867 in Ohio.

     vii.   WILLIAM FRIEND was born about Jun 1870.

     viii.   JAMES FRIEND was born about 1873 in Ohio.

     ix.   FANNIE FRIEND was born about 1876 in Ohio.

10.   JOSEPH[3] DELONG (Samuel Franklin[2], Abraham[1]) was born on 23 Apr 1839 in Laurel Township, Hocking County, Ohio. He died on 09 Dec 1891 in Goodhope Township, Hocking County, Ohio. He married Catherine Woltz, daughter of Thomas Woltz and Nancy Sutton on 01 Dec 1859 in Hocking County, Ohio. She was born on 03 Jul 1839 in Hocking County, Ohio. She died on 12 Dec 1929 in Lancaster, Fairfield County, Ohio.

More About Joseph Delong:
Occupation: 1860 in Laurel Township, Hocking County, Ohio; Farmer
Occupation: 1870 in Clear Creek Township, Fairfield County, Ohio; Farm
Laborer
Occupation: 1880 in Hocking Township, Fairfield County, Ohio; Farmer

More About Catherine Woltz:
Burial: 14 Dec 1929 in Fairview Methodist Church Cemetery, Good Hope Township, Hocking County, Ohio
Living In: 1900 Good Hope Township, Hocking County, Ohio
Living In: 1910 With her daughter, Alice, and her family in Good Hope Township, Hocking County, Ohio.
Living In: 1920 With her daughter, Alice, and her family in Good Hope Township, Hocking County, Ohio.

Joseph Delong and Catherine Woltz had the following children:

     i.   JOSEPH ALLEN[4] DELONG was born on 02 Aug 1862 in Ohio. He died on 30 Nov 1940 in Columbus, Franklin County, Ohio. He married (1) MARY ELLA STOWELL, daughter of Francis B. Stowell and Huldale Williams on 10 Sep 1908 in Franklin County, Ohio. She was born on 08 Feb 1862 in Iowa. She died on 29 Jan 1936 in Black Lick, Jefferson Township. Franklin County, Ohio. He married (2) MARY S HOEMAKER, daughter of Peter Shoemaker and Elizabeth Lefler about 1886. She was born on 13 May 1858 in Ohio. She died on 25 Mar 1907 in Etna Township, Franklin County, Ohio.

More About Joseph Allen Delong:
Burial: 02 Dec 1940 in Silent Home Cemetery, Reynoldsburg, Franklin County, Ohio

Notes for Joseph Allen Delong:
Buried beside his first wife.

----

   ii.   JAMES T. DELONG was born on 22 Jun 1865 in Hocking County, Ohio. He died on 29 Jun 1950 in Greenfield Township, Fairfield County, Ohio. He married (1) MARTHA ALICE DUDDLESON about 1888. She was born in Nov 1862 in Ohio. She died between 25 Apr 1930-06 Apr 1940. He married (2) DELLA JOHNSON, daughter of Ervin William Johnson and Nancy Botts between 25 Apr 1930-06 Apr 1940. She was born about 1886 in Pickaway County, Ohio. She died on 02 Feb 1968 in Lancaster, Fairfield County, Ohio.

More About James T. Delong:
Burial: 03 Jul 1950 in Amanda Township Cemetery, Amanda, Fairfield County, Ohio

   iii.   CHARLES H. DELONG was born on 10 May 1868 in Hocking County, Ohio. He died after 18 Apr 1940. He married (1) MARY ELLEN PRIMMER, daughter of Soloman A. Primmer and Eliza Carpenter on 22 Dec 1899 in Hocking County, Ohio. She was born on 13 Jun 1878 in Hocking County, Ohio. She died on 23 Aug 1913 in Columbus, Franklin County, Ohio. He married (2) FLORA ANDERSON, daughter of James Anderson and Etna Griffey on 08 Jul 1929 in Athens County, Ohio. She was born on 19 Jan 1899 in Bear Spring, Tennessee. She died after 18 Apr 1940.

More About Charles H. Delong:
Occupation: 1910 in Hocking Township, Fairfield County, Ohio; Railroad Car Inspector
Occupation: 1940 in Lancaster, Fairfield County, Ohio; Mould Polisher in Machine Shop

   iv.   IDA JANE DELONG was born on 10 Jul 1871 in Clear Creek Township, Fairfield County, Ohio. She died on 22 Jan 1927 in Hocking Township, Fairfield County, Ohio. She married ARTHUR A. CAMPBELL. He was born on 15 Apr 1860 in Hocking County, Ohio. He died on 07 Mar 1933 in Lancaster, Fairfield County, Ohio.

More About Ida Jane Delong:
Burial: 25 Jan 1927 in Forest Rose Cemetery, Lancaster, Fairfield County, Ohio Burial:

   v.   MARY E. DELONG was born on 03 Jan 1875 in Hocking Township, Fairfield County, Ohio. She died on 11 Dec 1949 in Lancaster, Fairfield County, Ohio. She married GEORGE YANTES. He was born on 03 Apr 1871 in Hocking County, Ohio. He died on

06 Mar 1953 in Lancaster, Fairfield County, Ohio.

More About Mary E. Delong:
Burial: 13 Dec 1949 in Forest Rose Cemetery, Lancaster, Fairfield County, Ohio

    vi.   EFFIE ALICE DELONG was born on 25 Dec 1877 in Fairfield County, Ohio. She died on 12 Aug 1958 in Hocking County, Ohio. She married William Jefferson Dupler, son of Seth Levi Dupler and Mary Ann Walker on 23 Dec 1900 in Hocking County, Ohio. He was born on 06 Nov 1873 in Good Hope Township, Hocking County, Ohio. He died on 30 Oct 1937 in Sugar Grove, Fairfield County, Ohio.

More About Effie Alice Delong:
Burial: Centenary Cemetery, Enterprise, Hocking County, Ohio
Living In: 1900 With her mother in Good Hope Township, Hocking County, Ohio.

11   CALISTA ANN[3] DELONG (Samuel Franklin[2], Abraham[1]) was born on 01 Nov 1841 in Laurel Township, Hocking County, Ohio. She died on 07 Aug 1901 in Ohio. She married JOHN F. THOMPSON. She married (2) MAURICE KANE on 17 Jun 1860 in Hocking County, Ohio. He was born on 23 Jul 1819 in Fairfield County, Ohio. He died on 02 Dec 1879 in Perry Township, Hocking County, Ohio. She married (3) JOHN ROTH between 15 Jun 1880-16 Mar 1884. He died before 23 Jun 1900.

More About Calista Ann Delong:
Burial: Betheny Cemetery, Buena Vista, Hocking County, Ohio
Living In: 1880 Perry Township, Hocking County, Ohio
Living In: 1900 With her son, George, and his family in Madison Township, Fairfield County, Ohio.

More About John F. Thompson and Calista Ann Delong:
Marriage License: 14 Dec 1858 in Hocking County, Ohio
Marriage Fact: Marriage license returned marked "annuled December 21, 1858".

More About Maurice Kane:
Burial: Betheny Cemetery, Buena Vista, Hocking County,
Ohio Cause Of Death: Consumption

Notes for Maurice Kane:
Headstone has 60 years, 4 months and 9 days for age at death. Death record has 60 years, 4 months and 28 days for age at death.

Maurice Kane and Calista Ann Delong had the following children:
    i.   HOWARD GRANT[4] KANE was born on 10 May 1869 in Perry Township, Hocking County, Ohio. He died on 21 Mar 1870 in Perry Township, Hocking County, Ohio.

    ii.   MINNIE B. KANE was born on 13 Mar 1871 in Perry Township, Hocking County, Ohio.

    iii.   GEORGE H. KANE was born on 28 Dec 1872 in Perry Township, Hocking County, Ohio. He died on 23 Feb 1943 in Lancaster, Fairfield County, Ohio. He married ROSA MAY (UNKNOWN). She was born on 21 Sep 1878 in Ohio. She died on 22 Jan 1969 in Ohio.

More About George H. Kane:
Burial: 26 Feb 1943 in Maple Grove Cemetery, Lancaster, Fairfield County, Ohio
Occupation: 1900 in Madison Township, Fairfield County, Ohio; Farmer
Occupation: Manager at Nehi Bottling Company

    iv.   ESTELLA L. KANE was born on 14 Jan 1875 in Perry Township, Hocking County, Ohio. She died on 17 Sep 1905 in Amanda Township, Fairfield County, Ohio. She married MARTIN LUTHER CONRAD. He was born on 18 Apr 1867. He died on 20 Apr 1951 in Ohio.

More About Estella L. Kane:
Burial: Amanda Township Cemetery, Amanda, Fairfield County, Ohio
Cause Of Death: Consumption

    v.   CHARLES CURTIS KANE was born on 23 Mar 1879 in Perry Township, Hocking County, Ohio. He died on 10 Nov 1933 in Columbus, Franklin County, Ohio. He married HARRIETTE (UNKNOWN). She died before 10 Nov 1933.

More About Charles Curtis Kane:
Burial: 13 Nov 1933 in Union Cemetery, Columbus, Franklin County, Ohio

John Roth and Calista Ann Delong had the following child:

    i.   CATHERINE[4] ROTH was born on 16 Mar 1884 in Madison Township, Fairfield County, Ohio.

12.   **MALINDA[3] DELONG** (Samuel Franklin[2], Abraham[1]) was born on 26 Mar 1844 in Laurel Township, Hocking County, Ohio. She died on 12 Jun 1920 in Wyandotte, Wayne County, Michigan. She married Louis L. Smyers, son of John Smyers on 03 Mar 1864 in Hocking County, Ohio. He was born on 23 Feb 1832 in Ohio. He died on 09 Sep 1915 in Wyandotte, Wayne County, Michigan.

More About Malinda Delong:
Burial: 15 Jun 1920 in Ferndale Cemetery, Riverview, Wayne County, Michigan

Notes for Malinda Delong:
Buried with her daughter, Ida, and Ida's husband. All three names are on the same headstone.

1841 is year of birth on headstone.

More About Louis L. Smyers:
Burial: Lancaster, Ohio
Occupation: 1870 in Perry Township, Hocking County, Ohio; Common Labor
Occupation: 1880 in Madison Township, Fairfield County, Ohio; Farm Laborer
Occupation: 1900 in Madison Township, Fairfield County, Ohio; Farmer
Occupation: 1910 in Madison Township, Fairfield County, Ohio; Retired
Military Service: Bet. 09 Aug 1861-20 Jul 1865 in Civil War; Company B, 31st Ohio Infantry, U.S. Army

Notes for Louis L. Smyers:

Mustered out of Company B, 31st Ohio infantry on July 20, 1865 at Louisville, Kentucky.

Louis L. Smyers and Malinda Delong had the following children:

      i.   WILLIAM[4] SMYERS was born about 1866 in Ohio.

      ii.   ELLSWORTH SMYERS was born on 15 May 1867 in Ohio. He died on 03 May 1938 in Liberty Township, Fairfield County, Ohio. He married ROSA (UNKNOWN).

           More About Ellsworth Smyers:
           Burial: Pine Grove Cemetery, Fairfield County, Ohio

      iii. ALMIRA SMYERS was born about 1868 in Ohio.

      iv. IDA BELL SMYERS was born on 24 Jun 1871 in Hocking Township, Fairfield County, Ohio. She died on 22 Jun 1941 in Wyandotte, Wayne County, Michigan. She married JOSEPH H. NYE. He was born in 1874. He died in 1957.

           More About Ida Bell Smyers:
           Burial: 25 Jun 1941 in Ferndale Cemetery, Riverview, Wayne County, Michigan

13.   JAMES[3] DELONG (Samuel Franklin[2], Abraham[1]) was born on 06 Jan 1847 in Laurel Township, Hocking County, Ohio. He died on 04 Mar 1912 in Pleasant Township, Fairfield County, Ohio. He married (1) ADIAN ANN CAVE, daughter of Michael Cave and Sarah Moore on 05 Jan 1867 in Hocking County, Ohio. She was born in Jun 1847 in Ohio. She died on 25 Dec 1933 in Derby, Darby Township, Pickaway County, Ohio. He married (2) MARGARETTA KANE, daughter of Maurice Kane and Elizabeth McDowell on 08 Mar 1874 in Fairfield County, Ohio. She was born on 07 Feb 1852 in Hocking County, Ohio. She died on 09 Jul 1938 in Lancaster, Fairfield County, Ohio.

More About James Delong:
Burial: 07 Mar 1912 in Saint Mathews Cemetery, Fairfield County, Ohio
Living In: 1870 With his brother, Joseph, and his family in Clear Creek Township, Fairfield County, Ohio.
Occupation: 1870 in Clear Creek Township, Fairfield County, Ohio; Farm Laborer
Occupation: 1880 in Amanda Township, Fairfield County, Ohio; Laborer
Occupation: 1900 in Pleasant Township, Fairfield County, Ohio; Laborer
Occupation: 1910 in Pleasant Township, Fairfield County, Ohio; None

More About Adian Ann Cave:
Burial: Pleasant Cemetery, Mount Sterling, Madison County, Ohio

More About Margaretta Kane:
Burial: 13 Jul 1938 in Saint Mathews Cemetery, Fairfield County, Ohio
Living In: 1920 Lancaster, Fairfield County, Ohio
Living In: 1930 Lancaster, Fairfield County, Ohio

James Delong and Margaretta Kane had the following children:

      i.   WILLIAM[4] DELONG was born about 1875 in Ohio.

           More About William Delong:
           Living In: 1930 With his mother in Lancaster, Fairfield County, Ohio.

Occupation: 1930 in Lancaster, Fairfield County, Ohio; Hotel Laborer

    ii.   MAGGIE E. DELONG was born on 19 Mar 1877 in Fairfield County, Ohio.

    iii.   EDNA DELONG was born about 1878 in Ohio.

    iv.   CLARA V. DELONG was born on 24 May 1883 in Fairfield County, Ohio.

    v.   BESSIE M. DELONG was born in Sep 1886 in Ohio.

    vi.   MAMIE L. DELONG was born in Jun 1890.

    vii.   JOHN F. DELONG was born on 07 Aug 1892 in Lancaster, Fairfield County, Ohio.

14.   **MINERVA JANE**[3] **DELONG** (Samuel Franklin[2], Abraham[1]) was born on 19 Mar 1852 in Laurel Township, Hocking County, Ohio. She died on 02 Oct 1915 in Lancaster, Fairfield County, Ohio. She married (1) **JAMES RAYMOND** on 29 Nov 1868 in Hocking County, Ohio. He was born about 1847 in Ohio. She married (2) **ELIAS POTTS** on 23 Oct 1877 in Fairfield County, Ohio.

More About Minerva Jane Delong:
Burial: Amanda Township Cemetery, Amanda, Fairfield County, Ohio

More About James Raymond:
Living In: 1860 With Caleb Hedges and his family in Perry Township, Hocking County, Ohio.
Occupation: 1870 in Laurel Township, Hocking County, Ohio; Farm Laborer

James Raymond and Minerva Jane Delong had the following child:

    i.   WILLIAM H.[4] RAYMOND was born on 14 Sep 1869 in Hocking County, Ohio. He died on 24 Mar 1950 in Lancaster, Fairfield County, Ohio. He married EMMA A. (UNKNOWN). She was born in 1872. She died in 1943.

        More About William H. Raymond:
        Burial: 27 Mar 1950 in Forest Rose Cemetery, Lancaster, Fairfield County, Ohio